Winning with Difficult People

Second Edition

Arthur H. Bell and Dayle M. Smith

BARRON'S

All inquiries should be addressed to:
Barron's Educational Series, Inc.
250 Wireless Boulevard
Hauppauge, New York 11788

Library of Congress Catalog Card No. 97-10353

International Standard Book No. 0-8120-9894-3

Library of Congress Cataloging in Publication Data
Bell, Arthur H. (Arthur Henry), 1946–
    Winning with difficult people / by Arthur H. Bell and
Dayle M. Smith. — 2nd ed.
        p.   cm. — (Business success series)
    Includes bibliographical references and index.
    ISBN 0-8120-9894-3
    1. Conflict management.   2. Interpersonal relations.
3. Interpersonal conflict.   I. Smith, Dayle M.   II. Title.
III. Series.
HD42.B45 1997
650.1'3—dc21   97-10353
                                                        CIP

PRINTED IN HONG KONG
987654321

ACKNOWLEDGMENTS

This book springs from data, examples, and stories shared by hundreds of business leaders and followers at all levels of organizational life. To them, and to academic researchers in the fields of conflict resolution and effective communication, we pay tribute and express sincere thanks. Executives, managers, and workers at the following companies were particularly influential in shaping our vision of how difficult people can be understood more fully and brought into more productive and tolerable relationships: Lockheed, Price-Waterhouse, Ernst and Young, American Stores, Star-Kist, Bain & Company, Countrywide Credit Industries, Southern Pacific, Cost Plus World Markets, Global Technologies, U.S. State Department, Central Intelligence Agency, Colonial Williamsburg Foundation, IBM, Pacific Bell, Apple Computer, Sun Microsystems, Hewlett Packard, U.S. Coast Guard, AT&T, Cushman & Wakefield, Levi-Strauss, China Resources, Deutsche Telekom, and U.S. Customs.

Arthur H. Bell
Dayle M. Smith
McLaren School of Business
University of San Francisco

To Lauren Elizabeth, Madeleine Alexis, and Arthur James.

Contents

Introduction

Most experienced businessmen and women accept the wisdom of the "85-15" rule: 85 percent of a manager's success comes from the ability to deal with 15 percent of his or her people. John D. Rockefeller said it well: "The ability to work with people is as purchasable a commodity as coffee or sugar, but I'll pay more for it than any other ability under the sun."

This is a book about dealing successfully with the most problematic of people—those who make work and life miserable for those around them. We'll call them S.O.P.'s—Sources of Pain.

S.O.P.'s live all around us in business. Above us in the pecking order is the boss who isn't doing his or her job, but wants to tell us how to do ours. Next to us is the S.O.P. coworker who refuses to cooperate, understand, or even try. And below us may be one or more whining S.O.P.'s who can't seem to accomplish even the simplest task without hand-holding. S.O.P.'s can also be outsiders: our clients, government representatives, and suppliers.

These are the difficult people who make up perhaps only a fraction of our daily contacts but cause most of our frustration in and out of the workplace. They've been called "crazy-makers," "odd ducks," and many less printable names.

Assume for now (as many people in the business world must) that you can't afford to quit if you're working under an S.O.P.; that you can't get a transfer if you're working next to an S.O.P.; and that, for union reasons or some other reason, you can't summarily fire an S.O.P. working under you.

You have to deal with the S.O.P. successfully. But how?

The following pages answer that question in practical ways by drawing on insights from more than five hundred interviews with business executives, managers, and workers conducted during the past eight years and from the latest research on conflict resolution, interpersonal dynamics, and effective business communication. Our goal in this second edition, as it was in the first, is to provide easy-to-use tools for overhauling, or simply tuning up, those business relationships that misfire too often.

Although the focus of this brief book must be limited to struggles with difficult people in the work environment, the principles and techniques described here can also be applied successfully to personal as well as other professional contacts.

Chapter 1

Why Bother with Difficult People?

There *is* such a thing as a bad boy. Even after you've gone the extra mile to understand an S.O.P.'s rheumatism, errant teenage daughter, receding hairline, and rampant crabgrass, there's still the ugly, undeniable truth: this person is a real jerk.

And one that you have to work with, not just patiently but productively.

Why? Because your success and your company's may depend on it, as the following cases demonstrate. (Of course, the names of the managers involved have been changed. Their words, however, are verbatim.)

If the S.O.P. is your boss, your future in the company depends in large part upon his or her approval. We can fantasize about simply telling off a problem boss—"you can take this job and shove it," or words to that effect. But in the real world of mortgages, kids, and car payments, few of us are in a position to quit.

Linda Richfield, a Seattle wiring inspector, works for a major aerospace company and an S.O.P. "My boss thinks he's a drill sergeant in the Army, which in fact he was twenty years ago," she says. "He never speaks when he can shout. He has never, in my six years with this company, given a single compliment for a job well done. Some of my coworkers literally tremble when they're called into his office. Why don't I quit? Put it this way. My husband and I owe $105,000 on a two-bedroom town house we bought last year. Nikki, our youngest, will need $2,300 in orthodontia soon. And there's one aerospace company in town—the one I work for. So I put up with my boss as well as I can."

If the S.O.P. is your coworker, the quality and quantity of your own work may well depend on your working together as a team. Making one team member a pariah, even for the best of reasons, sets in motion a daily office soap opera of tempers and gossip. Personal vendettas get played out in unexplained slowdowns, "lost" papers, and political backstabbing. Work quality suffers, and the professional faces of all the players are soon daubed with the tar intended only for the outcast.

Says Paul Velasquez, who works in a Cleveland escrow office, "There were six of us who had to work side-by-side with a true sicko I'll call Ralph. In his first few weeks with the company he went out of his way to alienate each of us, either by directly insulting us or whispering behind our backs. Once he took it upon himself to tell our boss the names of people who were making personal phone calls from work.

"So we decided to blackball the guy—I mean, literally not talk to him unless we had to. But we learned the hard way that blackballing doesn't work. Behind the scenes, he managed to delay or confuse important escrows in a way that made each of us look bad. It could be as simple a move as 'forgetting' a vital phone message or making sure that an important file was misplaced. In a team office, any one player can lose the game for the rest."

It's tempting to simply fire an S.O.P. But the road to termination must first be paved with paper—lots of it, in some corporate and government environments. The fastest way to sabotage your career as a manager is to bring down on the company an expensive legal suit or labor action caused by a hasty firing. And, as often as not, justifiable grounds for termination aren't present. The S.O.P. does his or her job just adequately enough to avoid formal discipline, all the while enjoying the cat-and-mouse game called "Bug the Boss."

Natalie Edwards had such an employee under her supervision in the federal Customs Department. Says she, "Brenda, as I'll call her, came to me by transfer from the Commerce Department—a transfer I couldn't refuse for political reasons. She's one of those employees who wants each and every one of her job duties specified in advance. If it's not in the written job description, she won't do it. For example, I tried to send her sixty-five miles to Baltimore to lead a two-day training seminar for federal trainees in her area of expertise. She refused to go, because business travel and public speaking were not specifically mentioned in her job description. Would I like to can her tomatoes? You bet! But practically speaking, I can't. She's a federal employee, probably for life. I spend quite a bit of my time now searching for a place to transfer her."

From the company's point of view, you must learn to deal with difficult people for bottom line financial reasons. The Academy of Management estimates that a company spends 90 percent of a new employee's first-year salary in hiring and training expenses. In many fields in which finding competent people is difficult, such as accounting, computer science, and engineering, companies have had to face the reality that corporate beggars for employees can't be choosers when it comes to workplace attitudes and personalities. A jerk may not be the best person for the job, but he or she may be the only person.

Paul Underwood is general manager of a thriving software development company based in rural Michigan. "I try to support the actions of my division managers," he says, "but recently I had to countermand a bad decision on the part of my quality control manager. He didn't get along with one of his employees, an inspector step II who had been with the company for eighteen months. One Friday afternoon they got into an argument over 'attitude' and 'insubordination,' ending in the on-the-spot firing of the employee by the manager. On Monday morning I reinstated the employee, though in a different division to save a bit of face for the manager involved. No matter what his attitude, the employee's work record was at least average or better. I reminded the manager that the company spent $4,200 to move that employee here to the sticks, and an additional $12,000 in training. It would probably cost us twice that to find and train a computer-literate replacement to move up here. Bottom line: the company can't afford to lose employees doing even the minimum of their job requirements."

In addition, there is the "gadfly" phenomenon in American business and professional life. The least likable or most maddening employee sometimes turns out to be dead right in his or her criticism of company policies, procedures, or production. These people regularly receive the spite of their fellow workers—until a whale of a problem looms up and they can say to one and all, "I told you so." Companies who know themselves to be well supplied with yes men and women have good reason to tolerate and even encourage the voices in the wilderness.

"I felt like firing her a thousand times," admits insurance executive Jerry Nielson. "She was a perpetual wet blanket on some of the most innovative, exciting programs we've developed in the company. No one wanted to work with her. She had that sour, you're-all-idiots expression and attitude. She also had an annoying habit of being right. Her statistical objections to our motorcycle insurance proposal probably ended up saving the company ten million dollars or more. When she left the company last year to take a better job with a competitor, we all breathed a sigh of relief. But there are many days now that we wish she were looking over our figures with that disgusted, impatient way of hers."

Whether they are bosses, coworkers, or subordinates, the S.O.P.'s in our business lives *do* bother us. But we sometimes overlook the many ways in which we bother them right back, often to our own disadvantage.

OUR USUAL WAYS OF TREATING S.O.P.'S

Notice how we usually interpret the workplace drama of personalities. The majority of us, the "good guys," get along well and consider ourselves a family of sorts. The S.O.P., as the social outsider, is seen as an aggressor—an active force attacking the relatively passive majority, the "victims." We communicate this view of the S.O.P. in the language we use to describe him or her:

> *"He makes me so mad."*
> *"He drives me crazy."*
> *"She ruins my whole day."*

There we have half of the drama of workplace conflict—the aggressor S.O.P. attacking the Happy Work Family. But it's only half the story. What are members of the Happy Work Family doing in response? The usual answers are lies: "We didn't do *anything* to him." "We were just minding our own business."

In fact, the drama of conflict involves both attack and counterattack. Understanding what we do in response to the actions or attitudes of S.O.P.'s is the first step in learning to deal with them successfully.

> *Face up to your own aggression toward difficult people.*

"But I swear I didn't do anything to him." Yes and no. Yes, you probably didn't act out your frustration or hostility in socially unacceptable ways (the ways chosen by the S.O.P.). But no, you were not passive in response to the S.O.P. In at least three strategic ways, you counterattacked:

NATURAL REACTION 1
WE STRIP THE S.O.P.

We commit our own interpersonal aggression by stripping the S.O.P. of virtually all positive attributes. The capable coworker who insults us is reduced to "that idiot—he's completely useless!" The fair but hard-nosed boss who crosses us suddenly becomes "a jerk who plays favorites." The longtime employee who begins to nettle us is cast as "my worst hiring mistake."

And, stung by pain inflicted by the S.O.P., we believe utterly in the reality of our newly created Straw Man. We're blinded to any redeeming qualities in the S.O.P. by the glare of hurt and anger.

So what? Doesn't the S.O.P. deserve what he or she gets? After all, we didn't start this row. We were just playing contentedly with the Happy Work Family when . . .

That scenario—so familiar to those of us who while growing up had brothers and sisters to blame—has grown threadbare and unproductive in the business arena. The issue is not what the S.O.P. deserves, or who is to blame. *The issue is how you can achieve your goals in spite of, and often by means of, the S.O.P.*

By recognizing our emotional tendency to strip the S.O.P. of all redeeming characteristics, we put ourselves in a proactive, not reactive, relation to the difficult person. We're able, in the situation, to act in our best interest without the blinding influence of emotional response alone.

Here's a brief case in point. Patricia Yard manages a highly successful Boston advertising office. Her mercurial executive assistant, Robert Isley, helps her keep up her breakneck work schedule. "We found ourselves slammed late one Friday by copy deadlines for two projects," says Yard. "I asked . . . well, I *told* Robert we would all be staying late into the evening. I was amazed when he got red in the face and told me bluntly that it just wouldn't be possible for him to stay late. Whammo! Like a bolt, my anger flashed strong negative judgments about him: 'disloyal,' 'ungrateful,' 'selfish,' 'unprofessional.' "

"In that one moment I had managed to blot out more than three years of faithful service by the best assistant I've ever had. I also was deaf to his explanation. All I wanted to hear was, 'Yes, boss, I'll stay.' He ended up staying that evening, but I lost him a month later to a competitor. He said he didn't like the pressure of the office."

NATURAL REACTION 2
WE DEFAME THE S.O.P.

Having stripped the difficult person of all positive qualities, we commit further interpersonal aggression by building consensus against the individual. Over coffee or lunch, we air our grievances to any and all who will hear. We ask about their experience with the individual, with the strong implication that we want to hear "the dirt." We bring up past events involving the S.O.P., putting him or her in as unfavorable a light as possible.

We know we can count on the Florence Nightingale predisposition among our fellows when we tell of our many wounds at the hands of the S.O.P. It feels good, in addition, to hear a growing chorus of complaints against the offending person.

The net result of this group therapy, unfortunately, is to blind us further to our interests with regard to the S.O.P. We become more convinced than ever of the justice and wisdom of our strong emotional reactions. How could we be wrong with so many coworkers affirming our outrage? "A fight in the streets is a regrettable thing," wrote the poet Keats, "but the energies displayed in it are fine." When they sense an impending fight to watch, our coworkers are often not a little gleeful to cheer on the combatants—both combatants, irrespective of who's right and who's wrong. La Rochefocault said it best: "There is something in the misfortune of our friends that does not entirely displease us."

Resist the temptation, therefore, to defame the S.O.P. This response only pollutes a potential source of objectivity, balance, and good advice: the uncoached opinions of your coworkers, freely expressed without request or influence from you. In short, how do your coworkers view your conflict with the S.O.P.? You'll never know if you set out on a campaign to defame the difficult individual.

In Miami last summer, we spoke at length with a group of managers about the defamation response. One manager said he understood the concept but didn't believe he was guilty of it. We asked him to keep track of his next conflict with a difficult coworker, and to report back to the group on his reactions.

"I had a run-in with a company vice president over a report she had assigned," he later told us. "She claimed that the report was due on her desk a week before the date she had actually given me. She kept insisting she was right. In the next day or two, I was amazed at how often her name came up in my conversation. I brought her up at coffee, at lunch, at home with my wife, and even at a dinner party with friends. It was as if I was hungry to tell someone—anyone—about how unfair this vice president was."

NATURAL REACTION 3
WE EXPLAIN THE S.O.P.

You're trying to install a new accounting procedure for the office, and one of your senior accountants is bucking you all the way. She has dozens of questions and objections. You know exactly what her problem is. She's one of the carryover employees from the days here when the ever-popular Walt Rogers had your position. You decide that she just can't adjust to the fact that you, not Walt, are in charge. Although she hasn't mentioned his name, you know that she's talking about how Walt would have done it.

Faced with interpersonal conflict, we all tend to ascribe motives to our opponent. Interestingly, we never ascribe benevolent or reasonable motives, only those that make our opponent seem narrow, self-serving, vengeful, or stupid.

In the case described above, the senior accountant in actual fact is objecting to the new accounting system because, in her opinion, it won't work well. Consider the positive motives we could ascribe to her objections:

1. She cares about the company and wants what's best.

2. She takes pride in her expertise and doesn't hesitate to voice it.

3. She wants to help her boss avoid a costly and embarrassing business mistake.

But we pass over these possibilities for the more tempting list of negative motives:

1. She's been waiting for a chance to criticize me in front of others.

2. She thinks she should have been promoted to Walt's old position instead of me.

3. She compares me unfavorably to Walt.

In attributing motives to the difficult person, we too easily create a monster from the cloth of our own insecurities. In the case above, the manager felt less than secure in his new position and feared any comparison with a previous boss, Walt, who was liked and respected by the employees. This manager will never get beyond those insecurities as long as he insists on interpreting every question and objection from employees as a challenge to his position and authority.

It's more helpful, and certainly more strategic, to begin with a blank slate in interpreting conflict with an S.O.P. There's solid wisdom in saying at the outset, "*I don't know* why she's acting the way she is." That stance leaves you the flexibility to take an obvious but often overlooked step: to ask the S.O.P. what motivates his or her actions. Chances are at least 50/50 that the S.O.P. will tell you his or her motives. Understanding that background, you will be much more likely to respond rationally and perhaps even sympathetically.

SUMMING UP

1. Sources of Pain are not a figment of your imagination. They do exist at all levels of organization life.

2. However, we tend to misunderstand S.O.P.'s by focusing solely on what *they* do, not what *we* do in response to their words and actions.

3. We often amplify the influence of S.O.P.'s by stripping away their positive attributes and overemphasizing their negative characteristics.

4. We spread the word about the S.O.P.'s words and actions. In the process, we ensure a no-win situation in which the S.O.P. cannot make a turnaround and we cannot back down from our positions as critics.

5. We make up myths to account for the behavior of the S.O.P. These myths usually support our point of view but may have little to do, in reality, with explaining the S.O.P.'s words and actions.

Chapter 2

Why Do Certain Types of People Bug Me?

One of the most influential tools for interpersonal success in business are the psychological theories of Carl Jung. In 1921, Jung proposed the "type" theory—that is, that each of us is predisposed to certain personality tendencies, which Jung arranged in four dimensions. Some individuals, Jung says, are by nature more extroverted, some more introverted. Some spend their energy handling details while others try to grasp the big picture. Some are predominantly logical, some emotional. Some are data gatherers, while others draw conclusions.

Within this range of personality attributes lie the seeds for most interpersonal conflict in business. It's easy to understand how an individual set upon making decisions can be frustrated by the efforts of a coworker to ferret out more and more details. A manager who operates through logic and objectivity can be driven up the wall by a fellow manager who wants to proceed using seat-of-the-pants intuition or heart-of-hearts emotion.

Jung's insights were extended and formalized by Katherine Briggs and Isabel Briggs Myers, developers of the Myers-Briggs Type Indicator; by David Keirsey and Marilyn Bates, in the Keirsey Temperament Sorter; and by others.

We offer our own easy-to-score instrument, based on the insights of Jung. We call it the Bell/Smith Personality Assessment.

Here's how this evaluation works. You enter your "a" or "b" choices on the scorecard after the questions. You can then use your results to understand more deeply your own personality predispositions and tendencies.

Why get to know yourself? Because only then can you understand why certain other personality types are difficult for you. Once you've scored the questions to determine your top four personality tendencies, you can use the following descriptions to understand in detail how these tendencies influence your business life.

(By the way, if you're shy about taking personality tests, you're not alone. Many people don't like tests of any kind, especially when the results will be compared with others' results. But take heart: the Bell/Smith Personality Assessment is simply a quick, general guide to some of your most basic habits of mind. You can't fail the test and you can't ace it—and neither can any of your coworkers.)

The Bell/Smith Personality Assessment will help you recognize *four* aspects of your personality and behavior from these possibilities:

THE MEMBER (M)

This personality trait predisposes you to enjoy the company of others. The Member joins groups willingly, seeks ways to include others in activities, and may tend to avoid tasks that must be accomplished alone. The Member relies on the consensus of the group for important decisions and may hesitate to form or express personal opinions without having them validated first by the group. The Member derives emotional strength and support from belonging, popularity, and the respect of others.

THE SELF (S)

This personality trait predisposes you to individual initiation and solitary work habits. The Self joins groups only for a compelling reason, and even then only for the period of the task at hand. The Self looks with suspicion upon widely held opinions and group-think. When faced by tasks too extensive or difficult for a single person to accomplish, the Self opts to divide work tasks into portions that can each be managed by individuals. The Self derives emotional strength from measuring up to personal standards, not the judgment of others.

member   self   juggler   planner

thinker   empathizer   closer   researcher

THE JUGGLER (J)

This personality trait predisposes you to minute-by-minute, seemingly practical adjustments to changing conditions. The Juggler manages to keep many tasks in progress at once, all in a partial state of completion. The panic of impending deadlines and the unpredictability of interruptions and emergencies are all energizing and challenging for the Juggler. It is a matter of pride to the Juggler that he or she can "handle" situations, "cope," and eventually see projects through to fulfillment. The Juggler derives emotional strength from a sense of sustained busy-ness as well as a conviction of his or her specialness and value to the group.

THE PLANNER (P)

This personality trait predisposes you to place details, individual facts, and other data into patterns. The Planner then clings to these patterns tenaciously, for they serve to organize an otherwise bewildering array of discrete items. The Planner is resistant to receiving disorganized data before a plan has been developed; but after the planning stage, he or she welcomes information, particularly insofar as it supports the designated plan. The Planner derives emotional strength from a conviction of his or her usefulness, as a shaping influence, on disorderly projects and groups. To a degree, the Planner also derives emotional strength simply from the nature of the plan developed—its symmetry, scope, and interrelation of parts.

THE THINKER (T)

This personality trait predisposes you toward finding, or attempting to find, logical links between thoughts, ideas, concepts, facts, details, and examples. The Thinker insists on postponing action until he or she "figures out" the underlying causes, effects, and relative accuracy or truth of mental propositions and assertions.

When in a data gathering mode, the Thinker is intent on "knowing more"; but when in assimilation and ratiocinating modes, the Thinker may reject or postpone new input of any kind. The Thinker derives emotional strength from the satisfaction of reaching logically defensible solutions to problems. Whether anyone acts on the basis of those solutions is less important to the Thinker than the success of the mental processes involved in arriving at them.

THE EMPATHIZER (E)

This personality trait predisposes you to focus on the emotional content of situations, as experienced personally or by others. The Empathizer appraises new information or a new situation first according to its emotional potential: How do I feel about this? How do others feel? Who will be hurt? Who will be happy? The answers to these questions play a prominent role in shaping the Empathizer's eventual point of view and action regarding the new information or situation. The Empathizer derives emotional strength from his or her self-image as a sensitive, caring individual and, often, from the gratitude and friendship of those targeted for his or her empathy.

THE CLOSER (C)

This personality trait predisposes you to make conclusions, judgments, and decisive acts (sometimes contrary to established procedures). The Closer is generally impatient with delays urged by others for additional thought, research, or planning. The Closer often grants that the whole truth is not known, but argues that enough of the truth is available for decision making. This personality type can be deaf to input that does not contribute directly to finalizing projects and processes. The Closer derives emotional strength from his or her reputation in the group as an action-oriented, no-nonsense decision maker and from the satisfaction of having used power and daring to manage difficult problems and personalities.

THE RESEARCHER (R)

This personality trait predisposes you to postpone judgment and action so long as it is possible to acquire new information. The Researcher craves certainty and suspects conclusions reached without consideration of all the evidence. The Researcher frequently ignores both time and resource constraints in pressing on with the search for additional data. In communicating that data to others, the Researcher may not be able to successfully organize and summarize the data gathered, since these activities both involve the drawing of tentative conclusions. The Researcher derives emotional strength from the treasure hunt excitement of investigation, from the strong influence his or her findings have upon eventual planning, and from the admiration of the group when such findings are announced.

Before determining where you may fit in these personality categories, try a brief experiment with one or more friends or coworkers. Photocopy the following list of questions and have each participant use it as an answer sheet. Allow each participant to have access to the eight personality-type descriptions. Begin the experiment by having each participant choose a letter from the list of personality-type descriptions for each of the following:

As the sole owner of a company, I would choose type _____ for CEO.

As a vice president of the company, I would prefer to work for type _____ as CEO.

As a manager in the company, I would prefer type _____ as my fellow managers.

As a line employee in the company, I would prefer to work for type _____ as my manager.

As a secretary in the company, I would prefer to work for type _____ as a manager.

As a manager, I would prefer to have type _____ as my secretary.

I would prefer to have type _____ as my spouse or significant other.

I would prefer to have type _____ as my only child.

Now compare results. Where differences in responses occur, discuss reasons for your choices.

Finally, decide what these results can teach us about dealing successfully with difficult people. Do you understand how easily differing personality types can fall into conflict? The same person you've identified as an S.O.P. may have simultaneously branded *you* an S.O.P. In other words, interpersonal difficulty lies in the eye of the beholder.

DETERMINING YOUR PERSONALITY TYPE

The following instrument is intended to serve the reader as an approximate guide to his or her personality type. It should be used in conjunction with the Jungian types identified earlier in this chapter.

Directions: Read each question and allow your initial response to guide your answer. (In some cases, you may not have a strong preference for either answer. Choose the answer that you agree with most.)

1. In the workplace, do you prefer
   a. making social conversation with many people during the day?
   b. making social conversation with only a few people during the day?

2. In learning a new work skill, do you prefer to be trained by
   a. following a step-by-step set of instructions?
   b. grasping the big picture and trying your own approaches?

3. Do your work associates value you most for
   a. what you think (your rational abilities)?
   b. what you feel (your heart or intuitions)?

4. As you review major accomplishments by others in your industry, do you believe their achievements have been due to
   a. a lot of hard work and a little luck?
   b. a lot of luck and a reasonable amount of hard work?

5. In your work relationships, do you consider yourself
   a. popular with many people?
   b. popular with only a few people?

6. In considering a job change, would you prefer to hear about
   a. what employees at the new company are doing?
   b. what employees at the new company may be able to do in the future?

7. When a new worker enters your work environment, do you form impressions based on
   a. their appearance and actions?
   b. the way they make you feel when you are in their presence?

8. In making business purchases, do you select items
   a. after careful comparison shopping?
   b. quickly, because you know what you want?

9. At work do you prefer jobs that
   a. bring you in contact with many people during the day?
   b. bring you in contact with few if any people during the day?

10. Do you consider speculation about unidentified flying objects (UFOs)
   a. childish and foolish?
   b. reasonable and interesting?

11. In managing others, would it be most important for you to be
   a. firm?
   b. friendly?

12. In arranging business deals, would you tend to
   a. spell out all details, even seemingly trivial ones, in writing?
   b. spell out major points of agreement and leave some details to good faith between the parties?

13. At work do you consider yourself to have
   a. many friends?
   b. few if any friends?

14. Do you think company leaders should be
   a. informative?
   b. imaginative?

15. When a coworker confides in you about a personal problem, do you tend at first to
   a. try to offer a possible solution?
   b. feel and express sympathy?

16. In superior-subordinate relationships at work, should duties and loyalties between the parties be
   a. stated clearly in written or spoken form?
   b. left partially unstated to allow growth and flexibility?

17. When meeting a new employee, do you tend to
   a. take the initiative in showing warmth and friendliness?
   b. wait for him or her to show signs of friendliness?

18. Should children be raised to
   a. learn real-world skills and behaviors as soon as they are ready?
   b. enjoy childhood freedom and fantasies as long as possible?

19. In work relationships, is it more dangerous to show
   a. too little emotion and personality?
   b. too much emotion and personality?

20. In designing interview questions for use in hiring a manager, would you tend to create
   a. questions with definite answers?
   b. questions that are open ended?

21. An old acquaintance (but not a good friend) unexpectedly encounters you in the lobby of a convention hotel. Do you tend to find this chance meeting
   a. enjoyable?
   b. somewhat uncomfortable?

22. In choosing artwork to hang on company walls, would you tend to choose paintings that
   a. communicate a single clear impression and meaning?
   b. communicate many possible impressions and meanings?

23. In deciding which candidate to support for a leadership position in your company, would you favor
   a. an intelligent, cool-headed candidate?
   b. a passionate and well-intentioned candidate?

24. Do you prefer social get-togethers that are
   a. planned?
   b. spontaneous and largely unplanned?

25. In going out to lunch with coworkers, would you prefer to eat with
   a. many coworkers?
   b. one or two coworkers?

26. Presidents of companies should be thoroughly
   a. practical.
   b. aware.

27. A former employee at your company is passing through your city and wants to stop by to say hello. Would you prefer that she
   a. make specific time and place arrangements with you in advance of her trip?
   b. call you on the spur of the moment when she arrives?

28. When attending a company social event taking place at 8 P.M., do you tend to
   a. arrive right on time?
   b. arrive somewhat later?

29. In making business phone calls, do you
    a. make most of the conversation, allowing little time for the other person to speak?
    b. spend most of your time listening and commenting briefly on what the other person is saying?

30. In moments of leisure, would you prefer to read
    a. a letter to the editor in a news magazine?
    b. a famous poem?

31. In choosing movies, do you tend to select
    a. movies that reveal social conditions and historical periods?
    b. movies that produce laughter or tears?

32. In preparing to be interviewed for a job, do you think you should prepare to talk more about
    a. your achievements?
    b. your future goals and plans?

33. If forced to accept dormitory accommodations during a conference, would you prefer to stay in a room
    a. with a few other compatible conference participants?
    b. alone?

34. In making work decisions, are you most influenced by
   a. the facts of the situation at hand?
   b. your feelings about the situation at hand?

35. In hiring employees to work for you, should they be primarily
   a. intelligent and creative?
   b. loyal and hardworking?

36. In purchasing real estate, it is more important to
   a. be ready to snap up a good deal before it disappears.
   b. have thorough knowledge of available properties.

37. In making a consumer complaint, would you prefer to
   a. call the company and talk to a customer representative?
   b. write to the company?

38. When performing an ordinary work task, do you prefer to
   a. do it the way it's usually done?
   b. try something new?

39. In court, judges should
   a. follow the letter of the law.
   b. show leniency or strictness where they think it appropriate.

40. When given a project to complete, would you prefer someone to give you
   a. a set deadline?
   b. the freedom to turn the project in when you feel it is ready?

41. When introducing two work associates who do not know each other, do you tend to
   a. tell them each a bit of information about the other to facilitate conversation?
   b. let them make their own conversation?

42. Which is worse for a manager?
   a. To be too idealistic.
   b. To be too much in a routine.

43. When you listen to a business presentation, do you prefer a speaker
   a. who proves his or her points with data and specific examples?
   b. who communicates excitement for and deep commitment to the topic?

44. At the end of the work day, do you spend more time thinking about
   a. what you did during the day?
   b. what you are going to do the next day?

45. In planning your ideal vacation, would you choose a place where
   a. you can meet with family and friends?
   b. you can be alone or with only one or two family members or friends?

46. At work, which mental activity appeals to you more?
   a. Analysis.
   b. Prediction.

47. Which would be more important to you if you were president of a company?
   a. That all employees understand their job responsibilities thoroughly.
   b. That all employees feel part of the company family.

48. As a member of a project team, would you prefer to be most involved in
   a. the completion stage in which final details are wrapped up?
   b. the initial conceptualization in which approaches are debated?

49. In learning a new work skill, would you prefer to be taught
   a. as part of a small class?
   b. one on one by a trainer?

50. If you had just two novels to choose from for leisure reading, would you be more likely to select
   a. the historical novel?
   b. the science fiction novel?

51. When you consider your career path, do you believe you should
   a. plan career moves months or years in advance?
   b. go with the flow of opportunities as they arise?

52. In paying tribute to a retiring company leader, should you focus primarily on
   a. the person's achievements?
   b. the person's aspirations?

53. Do you think the main purpose of meetings in business is
   a. getting to know one another and building team spirit?
   b. getting work done as efficiently as possible?

54. Are you most adept at
   a. drawing conclusions from facts?
   b. raising speculative questions?

55. The most important quality that a workforce can have is
   a. a spirit of individual initiative.
   b. team spirit.

56. Which of the following words comes closest to describing your behavior at work?
   a. Easygoing.
   b. Workaholic.

57. If your employer wanted to honor you at a luncheon, would you prefer a luncheon attended by
   a. many company employees?
   b. your employer and one or two others?

58. In general, which quality has mattered more for highly successful companies?
   a. Common sense.
   b. Inspiration.

59. If you had to choose, which of these two things would be better to say about a retiring employee?
   a. That he or she was excellent at his or her job.
   b. That he or she cared deeply about coworkers.

60. In working on a team project, do you tend to
   a. move it along to completion before the due date?
   b. make sure team members have considered all relevant information?

Scoring

Transfer your answers as checks in the appropriate spaces below:

1a___ b___	2a___ b___	3a___ b___	4a___ b___
5a___ b___	6a___ b___	7a___ b___	8a___ b___
9a___ b___	10a___ b___	11a___ b___	12a___ b___
13a___ b___	14a___ b___	15a___ b___	16a___ b___
17a___ b___	18a___ b___	19a___ b___	20a___ b___
21a___ b___	22a___ b___	23a___ b___	24a___ b___
25a___ b___	26a___ b___	27a___ b___	28a___ b___
29a___ b___	30a___ b___	31a___ b___	32a___ b___
33a___ b___	34a___ b___	35a___ b___	36a___ b___
37a___ b___	38a___ b___	39a___ b___	40a___ b___
41a___ b___	42a___ b___	43a___ b___	44a___ b___
45a___ b___	46a___ b___	47a___ b___	48a___ b___
49a___ b___	50a___ b___	51a___ b___	52a___ b___
53a___ b___	54a___ b___	55a___ b___	56a___ b___
57a___ b___	58a___ b___	59a___ b___	60a___ b___

___ ___ ___ ___ ___ ___ ___ ___ TOTAL
 M   S   J   P   T   E   C   R

Add up the total number of checks for the a and b columns. Then for each pair of letters at the bottom of the columns circle the letter for the column containing more checks. You should circle four letters all together. These suggest dominant aspects of your personality. The letters refer to the eight personality descriptions presented earlier in this chapter.

HOW TO INTERPRET YOUR SCORES

Your totals on the scorecard will suggest relative tendencies toward four of the eight possible personality-trait predispositions. The higher the score, the more intense that trait in your total personality.

Why four dominant traits? None of us consistently acts in accordance with one personality pattern. Instead, various traits (such as those you've identified through the Trait Indicator) interact—often in unpredictable ways—to produce the whole personality known as you.

Let's say, for example, that you have identified yourself as a Member, a Juggler, an Empathizer, and a Closer. Read through the descriptions of those personality traits and reflect upon how those traits interact in your personality. Perhaps in times of stress, one or more traits come to the fore. Perhaps some traits are evident at home while others are dominant at work.

What do you gain from such reflection? You come to know your own predispositions more accurately—and, in so doing, prepare yourself to understand why you may find certain other personality types difficult.

USING YOUR PERSONALITY-TRAIT SCORES TO UNDERSTAND DIFFICULT PEOPLE

It would be futile to simply chart, in a crude way, which personality types don't get along. Your own experience would quickly give the lie to any such chart; some of your close friends—or even your spouse—may have personality traits diametrically opposed to your own. Opposites do sometimes attract, as the saying goes, and no personality test or type chart can predict with any reliability our choice of friends or foes.

But your personality-trait scores can be useful in helping you gain insight into why you may find a given person so difficult. If you admit that you are a confirmed Planner, for example, it probably will make sense to you that a particular Juggler at work—always a bit late, always in a rush, always disorganized—drives you crazy. If you admit that you are an Empathizer at heart, you can understand why a cold, calculating Thinker isn't your cup of tea.

In determining your own dominant personality traits, you put yourself in a position to understand, at a deeper level, your own preferences and dislikes in other people. Simply understanding why a particular person is difficult for you can make it easier to treat that person with patience and even some self-directed humor. In effect, you're saying to the difficult person, "I now know we're coming at this problem from very different perspectives. I'll try to see it from your strange world if you'll try to see it from my strange world." Difficulty, in short, is in the eye of the beholder.

Nowhere are personality and preference differences more easily observed than among bosses and their employees. Notice in the following study how differently employees and bosses answered the question "What matters most for job satisfaction?"

DON'T ASSUME THAT WHAT'S IMPORTANT TO YOU IS IMPORTANT TO YOUR EMPLOYEE

(priority ranking of factors important for job satisfaction)

	Employees Ranked...	Bosses Ranked...
Full appreciation of work done	1	8
Feeling of being in on things	2	10
Sympathetic help on personnel problems	3	9
Job security	4	2
Good wages	5	1
Interesting work	6	5
Promotions	7	3
Personal loyalty to coworkers	8	6
Good working conditions	9	4
Tactful disciplining	10	7

Source: A. I. LeDue, Jr., "Motivation of Programmers," Data Base, 1980, 3, p. 5.

SUMMING UP

1. Estimating personality differences can be a valuable tool in building complementary work teams and in choosing suitable individuals for particular positions.

2. Personality traits include the Member, the Self, the Juggler, the Planner, the Thinker, the Empathizer, the Closer, and the Researcher.

3. In times of stress, personality traits may shift dramatically. A Juggler, for example, may become an obsessive Planner under certain conditions.

4. Understanding one's own personality predispositions can aid in predicting and dealing constructively with personality opposites in the workplace. A Planner, for instance, is likely to conflict with a Juggler. Simply knowing that they differ in their approaches to work goes a long way in helping these individuals avoid or resolve conflict.

Chapter 3

An Alternative to Anger:

Active Listening

There's no denying it: difficult people can make us angry. We often choose anger, in fact, as our primary way of dealing with difficult people.

To test your potential for anger, see which response you would choose in the following scenario.

At Miller Merchandising, Inc., you supervise six employees. You've called an important meeting for 1:30 sharp. But your "problem child" employee, Vincent, waltzes in twenty minutes late without an excuse. He just smirks when other employees chide him about being late. In the meantime, you've put the meeting on hold waiting for him.

What would you do?

a. get mad at Vincent on the spot, in front of others

b. get mad at Vincent in private, after the meeting

c. write an angry memo in which you put Vincent on notice regarding his tardiness

d. communicate your angry feelings toward Vincent by the silent treatment, derogatory comments to others, and other means

e. other response

Which answer is right? It depends, of course, on circumstances, personalities, and purposes. But the more important question is whether anger is a productive way of dealing with difficult people. If you chose a, b, c, or d, there's a good chance that you're relying on anger in such situations, possibly to your disadvantage.

MGM—MANAGEMENT BY GETTING MAD

In dealing with difficult people in your organization, you probably want no more or less than any manager wants: to get each employee's best effort. And anger may seem to serve well as a motivator for such effort, especially with difficult types. Here's how a West Coast fabrics buyer describes his boss's angry management style:

"Around the office we think of him as Father, with a capital *F*. At the start of the day, he lets the whole office know that he's livid by shouting at his poor, long-suffering secretary. Or he takes what we call a 'huff walk' down the halls. As he strides by, he seems to be breathing fire over some undefined, galling offense. Throughout the day he communicates anger in many ways: a dyspeptic scowl, a refusal to listen, a brusque and sarcastic manner. Believe me, when he's aroused his language can peel wallpaper."

Does such behavior work in dealing with others? "Yes and no," says the fabrics buyer. "Yes, we do toe the line at work. We arrive exactly on time and never leave early. We keep our noses to the grindstone, or pretend to, when the boss is around. But no, his management style doesn't work long term. We all hate being around him. Six good employees quit last year just because of his outbursts and personal attacks. A lot of us are looking. Who needs it?"

WHY WE GET MAD

Ask angry managers who lit the fuse to their fireworks and they will point to difficult people and say something like "Their screwups would make anyone crazy!" Angry managers, in fact, often defend their anger on the grounds of company loyalty and commitment. "I feel like I'm the only one in my division who really cares about company goals," a Nordstrom manager says. "Too many of my employees are just thinking about their next paycheck."

In other words, anger is viewed by many managers as a red badge of courage—a sign that they're fighting for the company, with blood in the eye and bayonet mounted. *Fortune* and other business magazines encourage these attitudes by frequently publishing articles on the "Ten Toughest Bosses in America." Such articles lionize managers with flash tempers and thick skins. These are supposedly the "no nonsense" managers who "make the hard decisions."

THE LONG-TERM EFFECTS OF MANAGING BY GETTING MAD

Undeniably, managing others through anger does seem to work in the short term. Difficult employees learn to stay out of the angry manager's way. Everyone is "good" when the boss is watching.

But Rambo doesn't manage others well for long. Consider three inevitable results of relating to others through anger:

1. THE ANGRY MANAGER EXPLODES

Physically and emotionally, managers break down when, day in and day out, they attempt to manage by means of blood pressure and Maalox. Today's outburst has to be repeated, with even more intensity, tomorrow, and employees come to expect an "encore" to the boss's fits of rage. The boss finds himself or herself always having to up the ante on anger. What used to take only a harsh glance now requires a ten-minute tantrum.

Lee Iacocca had to face up to his inclinations toward anger in his career. "I was full of anger, and I had a simple choice: I could turn that anger against myself, with disastrous results. Or I could take some of that energy and try to do something productive. . . . It's always best to plow your anger and your energy into something productive."

Unchecked anger leads quickly to signs of managerial breakdown: persistent stomach cramps, heart arrythmias, general fatigue, increased smoking and drinking, and other widening cracks in the personality under stress. Underlining the dangers to health is the 1989 Dartmouth Heart Study, which pointed to the component of anger in Type A personalities as a prime contributor to hypertension, stroke, and heart attack.

2. GOOD EMPLOYEES QUIT

Bright people, even when they're difficult to work with, don't remain long in the employ of perpetually angry managers. Recent analyses of exit-interview data across industries show that good employees quit primarily because of interpersonal difficulties, not for financial reasons. One of the most common comments in exit interviews is "I just couldn't stand working for my boss."

3. THE BEST IDEAS ARE NEVER HEARD

An atmosphere of managerial anger sends employees into a "safe mode"—that no-risk form of behavior in which only approved and traditional thoughts and actions are undertaken. After all, who wants to call down the wrath of Khan?

As a consequence of this lack of communication, angry managers find themselves more and more alone during the business day. Few employees ask for conferences or meetings. Left to themselves, angry managers find more time to brood and to pick new locations for lightning to strike.

ACTIVE LISTENING AS AN ALTERNATIVE TO ANGER

Let's say you know in your heart of hearts that you, like Lee Iacocca, have at least a tendency to use anger as a way of managing others, including difficult people. What can you do to break this pattern of interpersonal behavior?

A Greek philosopher put it wryly: "The gods gave us two ears and one mouth. They should be used in that proportion."

Few of us listen carefully enough to what those we care about are saying—our closest friends, our spouses, our relatives. How much less likely, then, that we will hear even a small percentage of the real, whole message aimed at us by difficult people in our professional lives.

Frankly, we often don't want to know what they're saying. And when we're forced to listen, we make up our minds in advance about what "they're always on about." In other words, we hear through the distorting filter of our assumptions. And, not surprisingly, difficult people become even more difficult when they are misunderstood or ignored.

Active listening begins when we learn to adopt what Carl Rogers calls "an empathic attitude"—a willingness to be sensitive to the many levels of messaging that make up the whole message. Consider some of these levels:

◆ *The occasion for the message:* Why is the person contacting me now?

◆ *The length of the message:* What can length or brevity tell me about the importance of the message to the person?

◆ *The words chosen:* Is the message communicated in formal, aloof language? Impatient slang?

◆ *The volume and pace:* What can these tell me about the emotional pressure behind the message?

◆ *The pauses and hesitations:* How do these qualify or undercut the main message?

◆ *Nonverbal cues:* What can eye contact, posture, facial expression, and gestures tell me about the message?

Needless to say, no skilled listener goes down a checklist of items to assemble the whole message. These aspects of total communication are perceived and interpreted simultaneously—if the listener is aware of them.

In your next encounter with a difficult person try active listening. You may find the following three techniques helpful:

TECHNIQUE 1

At the outset, consciously turn off your prejudgments and assumptions about the conversation. Let it happen in the same way that you let a play or movie unfold. Try to ask more questions ("What do you mean?" "Tell me more about that." "Can you give me an example?") than you usually do.

TECHNIQUE 2

Repeat some of the person's key phrases and ideas as they occur in the conversation. Your tone should be one of interest, not judgment.

Speaker 1: So, as I told Mr. Wilson, I'm not going to be ridiculed in front of others for the way I dress at the office.

Speaker 2: Ridiculed . . .

Speaker 1: Well, what would you call it? He brought the subject up at our staff meeting and looked directly at me.

Speaker 2: Looked at you . . .

Speaker 1: Of course, he looked at other people as well, but I felt his remarks were aimed particularly at me.

As this conversation continues, the technique of repeating his words can be used to get the difficult person to express himself more accurately. Of course, it should be used discreetly.

Listening often suggests self-giving kindness—a form of interpersonal charity. But Walter Kiechel III, writing in *Fortune* magazine, points to three very selfish reasons to listen up. If you don't, Kiechel says,

◆ "you are liable to prove a poor negotiator. No win-win for you, baby, if you can't tune in to what the other fellow truly wants, or might settle for."

◆ "you leave yourself open to unpleasant, career-derailing surprises. . . . The higher you go, the more you wrap yourself in the mantle, the less likely your subordinates are to tell you bad news. To get the truth, you have to show them that you hear, and indeed welcome, the occasional discouraging word."

◆ "you will flunk crisis management. The experts say that under high stress, when you most need information, even a good listener's system will shut out incoming signals."

◆

David Burns, M.D., author of *The Feel Good Handbook,* explains the technique of active, empathic listening in this way: "The key is to put yourself in the other person's shoes and look for the truth in what that person is saying."

Not that it's easy. Dr. Burns tells of a recent listening challenge of his own. ". . . I was counseling a businessman named Frank who tends to be overbearing when he's upset. Frank told me that I was too preoccupied with money and that he shouldn't have to pay at each of our sessions. He wanted to be billed monthly.

"I felt annoyed because it seemed Frank always had to have things his way. I explained that I had tried monthly billing, but it hadn't worked out because some patients didn't pay. Frank argued that he had impeccable credit and knew much more about credit and billing than I did.

"Suddenly I realized I was missing Frank's point. 'You're right,' I said. 'I'm being defensive. We should focus on the problems in your life and not worry so much about money.'"

"Frank immediately softened and began talking about what was really bothering him, which were some personal problems. The next time we met, he handed me a check for twenty sessions in advance!"

TECHNIQUE 3

Take a moment to jot down what you remember after your next conversation with a difficult person. This exercise, which should take just a minute or two, will pay dividends in sensitizing you to the "headlines" contained in what others say. Even in the act of listening you'll be trying to pick out the major points instead of rushing ahead to general impressions. You will probably notice that you're listening more carefully after doing this exercise only three or four times.

SUMMING UP

1. Anger is a natural but often unproductive emotion in dealing with difficult people.

2. Those who attempt Management by Getting Mad run several risks:

   ◆ Good employees quit rather than endure the antics of the angry manager.

◆ The angry manager suffers physical and emotional ailments.

◆ The best ideas do not surface in an atmosphere of anger and punishment.

3. Angry responses can be replaced by the more productive techniques of "turning off judgmental voices," "repeating key messages," and "jotting down headlines" of what others communicate to you.

Chapter 4

Winning with Twelve Difficult Types

In this chapter, we will apply our discussion of personality types to twelve S.O.P.'s found in the business world. We will assume these people work for you or with you, but their characteristics can apply to those you work for as well. In each case, we will 1) describe the difficult person in detail; 2) consider strategies for dealing successfully with him or her; and 3) review an actual business situation in which the difficult person was brought into tow.

A MODEL FOR VISUALIZING DIFFICULT TYPES

The grid on page 51 is surprisingly simple to interpret. It suggests that difficult people find themselves placed somewhere on the horizontal axis between complete isolation and complete involvement with other people in the company. Further, these difficult people can simultaneously be placed along the vertical axis from virtual silence (actions speak only by implication) to nonstop verbalizing (complete explanation or explication of opinions and positions).

Let's read the placement of difficult people on this grid like a Hebrew book, from right to left, top to bottom. The twelve most common S.O.P.'s in the business arena can be arranged along these coordinates:

	Confederation (involvement with others)			Isolation
Explication (verbal explanation)	4	3	2	1*
	5	6	7	8
Implication (nonverbal demonstration)	12	11	10	9

Numbers refer to difficult types described in this chapter.

S.O.P. NO. 1
THE VOICE CRYING IN THE WILDERNESS

This difficult person is almost completely isolated in the company, but sounds forth nevertheless with a flood of memos ("I want to bring to your attention . . ."), phone calls ("I thought you should know that . . ."), and letters to the company newsletter ("Management has again deceived workers by . . ."). The Voice speaks as if representing a large employee power block; in actual fact, he or she sits stewing all alone in a small office somewhere in the company, contemplating where lightning should strike next.

Most employees in the immediate vicinity of the Voice quickly learn to ignore his or her rampages. But managers can find this S.O.P. both irritating and destructive, especially when the Voice sends anonymous messages to senior corporate officers, government regulatory agencies, and public interest groups.

Like most difficult people, the Voice draws a road map to his or her Achilles heel by word and action. The Voice is looking for an audience. The more people in the company ignore the messages of the Voice, the more strident and daring he or she becomes in memos, calls, and letters. Conversely, the presence of even a small audience can mollify the Voice. Much of the anger that motivates the Voice's expressiveness may come from his or her social isolation in the company. That anger can be defused by welcoming the Voice as a member of a company social committee or other group.

Strategy: Thank the Voice for his or her informative communications, and ask that they be directed in the future to the executive committee (or general manager, employee relations committee, etc.). Make these audiences aware that they will be receiving regular, perhaps strange communications from the Voice, and thank them in turn for handling these messages patiently.

Strategy: Interpret the social isolation and anger of the Voice as a plea to be included in company social life. Structure the Voice's inclusion in social gatherings so he or she must attend regularly over an extended period of time. (This type of S.O.P. tends to give up quickly on any unstructured, voluntary social exposure.)

A Business Example

From a manager at a St. Louis military contractor: "Allen P. came to our company with $220,000 in his pocket from a settlement with a previous employer. He had blown the whistle there, justifiably, on illegal overruns on federal contracts. We hired him for his high degree of expertise in corporate tax accounting. From the beginning, however, Allen made it clear that he hated working with others. He used sarcasm and personal attacks to exclude himself from team projects. Within a few months, he was rarely seen outside of his office. However, he communicated regularly with senior management through a series of well-written, attention-getting memos.

"As Allen's immediate boss, I became increasingly uncomfortable with this sullen presence who 'told all' on an almost daily basis to my superiors. I was on the verge of calling Allen into my office and telling him to lay off the memos when I remembered his previous experience with whistle blowing. This man was tempting me to try to silence him. He was begging for me to make him a cause célèbre again, to put him on a stage where he could get more attention.

"I decided to oblige him, but in a way he didn't expect. A senior vice president and I made up the monthly 'Pulse Award,' for employees who went beyond the call of duty in keeping a finger on the pulse of the company, guarding against misinformation and mistakes. Needless to say, Allen was our first recipient, with appropriate hoopla in the company magazine. The attention seemed to give Allen what he wanted. He's warmed up to several people in the office. He and I talk through some of his concerns on a regular basis now, so he finds it less necessary to send his verbal torpedoes to senior management."

S.O.P. NO. 2
THE BACKSTABBER

This difficult person is less isolated but just as vocal as the Voice. The Backstabber builds temporary associations with other employees only to play them like pawns for personal advantage and advancement. Managers must act decisively to neutralize the Backstabber, who singlehandedly can kill team spirit and mutual trust.

The process of backstabbing typically works like this: Employees A, B, and C work closely enough over a period of time to become friendly and to drop protective defenses regarding their attitudes and preferences. Employee A reveals that he dislikes the boss. Employee B casually lets it drop that she is job hunting. At an opportune moment, Employee C makes the boss privy to both nuggets of information and, for his thirty pieces of silver, is set above the other two for raises and promotion.

Obviously, the activities of the Backstabber can't be rewarded in any way. On the contrary, a manager must play detective to find out who in the office is holding the bloody knife. This can be done most effectively by getting to know each employee well, perhaps by means of frequent brown-bag lunch get-togethers or breakfast meetings. When managers have established "trust links" to employees, any derogatory information received from a backstabber can be checked out by the manager quickly and confidentially by going directly to the employee concerned.

So much for repairing the damage caused by the Backstabber. But can he or she be reformed?

Consider the political sophistication of the Backstabber. Anyone that proficient at human gamesmanship has talents that should be channeled constructively. The key, as with the Voice, is to discover what the Backstabber wants. A simple one-on-one "career goals conference" with the manager can start the Backstabber on the road back to constructive participation in the work team. Given the manager's undivided attention to his or her aspirations, the Backstabber no longer has to stand on the bodies of others to get noticed. In such a conference, the manager can clue the Backstabber in to the basic culture of the company—a culture that values mutually supportive relations, not internecine conflict.

Strategy: Value team spirit among employees so highly and evidently that backstabbing is neither rewarded nor encouraged.

Strategy: Check out derogatory information quickly and privately to defuse the suspicion and ill will upon which the Backstabber depends.

Strategy: Discuss career goals with the Backstabber and communicate the unwritten rules of civilized behavior within the company's culture.

A Business Example

From a Dallas energy company vice president: "I think one of my employees had been watching *Dallas* on TV too much. He was at least as devious as J.R. in setting up other employees for failure, then miraculously coming to the rescue at the last moment. On one occasion, he talked me into giving a report writing assignment to three other employees in his group. I didn't realize that only he had access to the data they needed for the report. When the deadline came and they failed to produce, he came forward with his own report, which he said he 'threw together at the last moment.'"

"But the gambit backfired on him. Instead of praising him for saving the day, I read him the riot act for concealing data from the other employees. I turned over his report to them for revision. With the passing of time, his ruffled feathers have been smoothed out and the team is functioning smoothly. But I think he learned a valuable lesson about manipulating his fellow employees for his own advantage."

S.O.P. NO. 3
THE YES, BUT . . .

This difficult person is moderately involved with other employees, usually as their mouthpiece. The Yes, But . . . raises nitpicking objections to even the most straightforward task. The Yes, But . . . always seems to know a better way, a more logical approach, a cheaper alternative. Work stalls if a manager takes time to discuss each roadblock Yes, But . . . sets up. Nevertheless, the manager can't brush aside all feedback from employees. Good ideas and crucial warnings do come up to managers from the grassroots level.

The solution to the Yes, But . . . employee lies in forcing the full burden of objection upon him or her. Notice that "Yes, but . . ." is only the beginning of an objection. Too often a manager leaps in not only to defend his or her own position but to flesh out the objection itself. The Yes, But . . . employee quickly learns that even the hint of an objection will send the manager into defensive overdrive.

Shrewd managers continue to welcome the input of Yes, But . . . employees but insist that all such objections be put in writing. The act of writing requires that half-baked thoughts be filled out into sentences and then structured into a cogent argument with evidence and recommendations. The great majority of Yes, But . . . employees have neither the energy nor the commitment to develop their objections in this way. Only the most important of their quibbles will ever see the light of day on paper.

Strategy: Continue to encourage employee feedback, but require that Yes, But . . . objections to policies, procedures, and other matters be made in writing for thorough review.

A Business Example

From the founder of a Washington, D.C., consulting firm: "We have to act quickly to win consulting contracts. Our proposal-writing team often works around the clock at the office as deadlines near for important RFP's [requests for proposals]. Their work was slowed considerably last year by a former manager who wanted to play back-seat driver. Every move the writing team made or wanted to make was challenged by this manager. He never could suggest a better alternative, of course, but he had a steady stream of criticism for the ideas of others. As a result of his obstructions, we didn't complete our proposal on time for a multimillion-dollar computer literacy training program for the Department of Agriculture. He isn't working here anymore."

S.O.P. NO. 4
THE POLITICIAN

This, the most dangerous of all difficult people, has not only full expressive powers but also the attention, and sometimes the support, of many employees. The Politician seeks to position himself or herself as a power broker between management and labor. Paying court to the Politician in too obvious a way ensures his or her growing power base; ignoring the Politician creates a powerful adversary.

The solution to dealing with a Politician is to enfranchise other employee groups and spokespeople without overtly passing over the Politician. A Politician's power base is often held together not by his or her own network of favors, obligations, and friendships, but by the vacuum of managerial neglect. When a manager makes no regular contact with large numbers of employees, a Politician of some sort inevitably fills the void.

Enfranchisement of employee groups and spokespeople can come through invitations to important meetings, opinion surveys, reorganization of large employee blocks into smaller teams, and the use of quality circles and discussion groups. The dangers and difficulties posed by a power brokering Politician can be overcome not by challenging his or her influence directly but by dismantling his or her power base piece by piece.

Strategy: Avoid amplifying the power of a Politician by paying court or through direct confrontation.

Strategy: Defuse the power of a Politician by giving attention and influence to groups and individuals within his or her constituency.

A Business Example

From a New York publishing company: "As vice president and publisher of a large college textbook publisher, I faced an awkward situation some years ago with the forty or so developmental editors we employ. These men and women work directly with authors and manuscripts to prepare final drafts for typesetting. At that time, they were known, corporately, as low people on the totem pole in this company. I and my editor-in-chief had little direct contact with them.

"One day in late fall we were presented with a list of demands from our developmental editors. They were represented by one of their own, a tall woman we knew only by name and by her reputation as one of our best developmental editors. Our responses to the list of demands, she said, were to be delivered to her. She, in turn, would communicate them to the rest of the developmental editors.

"We faced a dilemma. To fire her as the ringleader of this mini-uprising would cost the company an excellent employee and risk the long-term anger of dozens of other developmental editors. Yet to comply with the request was to install her permanently as a quasi-union spokesperson in a distinctly nonunion environment.

"We tried a strategy that worked well. After thanking her for delivering the list of demands, we told her that we would consider them with care. The next day our department editors each called a discussion meeting with their own developmental editors. Each meeting produced its own list of grievances and suggestions, and these lists quickly took the place of the former list of demands as our agenda for action. As vice president, I took the step of appointing two developmental editors (not the woman presenting the original list) to the company's executive committee. We took other steps to ensure that developmental editors could make opinions heard as individuals and small groups. As a result, we never had to deal through a single individual or to haggle with employees over a single list of demands."

S.O.P. NO. 5
THE BUSYBODY

This difficult person is certainly involved with many people in the company, but doesn't express himself or herself as fully and credibly as the Politician. The Busybody never learned the wisdom of the World War II saying "Loose lips sink ships." The Busybody regularly (and often unintentionally) sabotages office morale and departmental planning with incessant "I-just-heard's."

Most Busybodies in corporate life are looking for attention and affection. They've learned to use information to gain entry to conversations and social relationships. The more harmful the information to coworkers or current projects, the hotter its value for the Busybody. In some offices, the route of the Busybody is fixed, and his or her gossiping visits come with the regularity of the lunch wagon.

Because the Busybody seeks social acceptance so desperately, his or her actions can be curtailed by the power of relationships. As in the following business example, a Busybody stops gossiping when he or she learns that important relationships—like the employer-employee relationship—depend on mutual trust. This truth can be communicated directly to the Busybody in a short conference.

Strategy: Make the Busybody aware of the damage that is done to personalities, projects, and planning when information is leaked prematurely or in a distorted manner. Remind the Busybody of the trust placed in him or her by management, and how important that trust is to ongoing business relationships.

A Business Example

From a manager of a Philadelphia knitting mill: "Our business, the knitting of caps, sweaters, socks, and ties, is a roller-coaster ride every year, depending on the buying patterns of big department stores and the impact of foreign competition. We're always either adding staff in a hurry or laying people off. We get nothing from our people, however, if they're constantly worried about rumors of layoffs.

"When layoffs were being considered last winter, a top-secret list of six possible employees to be laid off was somehow leaked throughout the company. I managed to track the leak to a clerk in the photocopy room. It turned out he was relatively new to the company, and used this information as a way to 'get in' with older employees.

"I sat him down and showed him the facts. First, the layoffs hadn't been necessary after all. Second, his gossiping had caused two of the six employees to accept employment with a competitor. Third, our managers had to spend many hours reassuring individual employees who had heard his rumors. I calculated that his gossip had cost the company well over $60,000 in lost labor, retraining, and other costs.

"I didn't fire him. He now understands that even the lower-echelon jobs in the company, like his in the copy room, carry with them a high degree of trust."

The psychological needs of the difficult person may exceed the time resources and personal counseling abilities of a manager. When that happens, it's a relief to call in a company counselor, such as Jon Lobe of the Bell Atlantic Employee Assistance Program. With a trained counselor, difficult employees can talk through issues at length. "They really want a place to rethink things verbally," says Lobe. "They need a place outside the normal structure." But few companies provide intensive one-on-one counseling support; for example, Lobe is responsible for making counseling available to any one of 8,000 Bell Atlantic employees. Managers and supervisors, Lobe says, are still the first line of defense against destructive conflict; as such, they "have to learn how to handle conflict, because it gets in the way of production."

S.O.P. NO. 6
THE SHORT FUSE

This difficult person usually has a moderate range of social contacts in the company and reasonably well-developed expressive abilities. God knows he or she has a temper.

The Short Fuse manipulates work associates (and sometimes managers) with the perpetual threat of a temper tantrum. This difficult person discovered early on that most people prefer to avoid highly emotional confrontations. Even those coworkers who don't care about whether the Short Fuse explodes would prefer not to be involved in a shouting match. The Short Fuse creates for himself or herself a comfortable work environment, because people step aside, make allowances, and avoid the dragon's breath.

Short of paying for intensive psychotherapy, we will probably not change the basic emotional style of the Short Fuse. But we can draw the line at the office door for such angry outbursts, much as we don't allow drinking on the job. The Short Fuse can be counseled to understand that his or her unmanageable anger is a) completely inappropriate for work relations, and b) won't earn him or her special treatment. Your company counselor can be helpful in setting up a planned approach to reducing the outbursts of the Short Fuse.

Strategy: Don't let the Short Fuse gain special advantages under the threat of a temper tantrum. Make the Short Fuse aware of what works and doesn't work in business relationships. Set up an ongoing program to change his or her behavior.

A Business Example

From a middle-level manager at a Southern California computer-graphics company: "I didn't believe that the squeaky wheel got the grease until I took a management position here two years ago. Twenty-two programmers and trainers report to me, and twenty-one of them are delightful people. Then there's Roberta. About once a month she was in the habit of getting into a top-of-the-lungs, screaming tantrum over some business problem or misunderstanding. Apparently, she had been doing this for a couple years before my arrival at the company.

"I was amazed at the 'space' she had created for herself by her temper. People thought twice about asking her to do anything, because she 'might explode.' The previous manager said he rarely criticized her work, because 'you know how she can be.' Roberta had managed to scare the entire office.

"During my first week as manager, I called her into the office, gave her three assignments I knew she didn't want, and pointed out some problems in a "C" program she had just completed. It was beautiful—she went off like a geyser. I listened to her tirade. When she simmered down, I went on in the same tone of voice, as if nothing had happened. She eventually left my office dumbfounded—and did her assignment very well.

"It took a couple more experiences like that over a period of months for Roberta to learn that her outbursts of anger were no more important to me than a sneeze. The only objections I would entertain were those delivered in a rational, civilized manner. To her credit, she got the point and we've worked well together ever since."

Consider this advice from a well-known management expert on how to deal with angry employees:

In his popular "Management Letter," Mortimer R. Feinberg, Ph.D., discusses the surprise of anger in the workplace.

"You may have developed expert mechanisms for handling family members when they overreact, but you're still at a loss when staffers behave that way—especially your top people." Feinberg recommends that you first simply let anger play itself out. "Don't interrupt while an employee is letting off steam. Venting anger will do him or her good and reduce the urgency of the moment." In addition, says Feinberg, show that you are listening intensely. "In these kinds of situations, the greatest sign of respect and sincere attention you can show an employee is simply hearing him or her out."

You may choose not to overreact, or to react at all, to an employee's angry outburst. But conflict among employees shouldn't be ignored. "I used to think it was better to ignore conflicts between staff members, let things ride, let people work things out among themselves," says Fraser Duke of Flint Hills Construction in Atlanta. "I found out the hard way that this doesn't work. People often can't work it out on their own, and it ends up costing the company time, productivity, and sometimes good people."

Many companies have built conflict control into the structure of their work weeks. John Davidson, vice president of Sherri-Lynn, Inc., a Georgia dress manufacturer, explains his company's program: "We were looking for a way to contain certain conflict, and we found it. This system has really paid off." At Davidson's firm, five randomly selected employees attend biweekly meetings with the personnel director, Davidson, or the company owner, Sol

Roberts. In advance, the names of the employees are posted so that others in the company can contact them with agenda items for meeting. Says Davidson, "We've seen results."

S.O.P. NO. 7
THE LIAR

This difficult person has burned most of his or her social bridges in the company and has relatively little expressive credibility. What the Liar does say is immediately discounted by others who know his or her deceiving ways. The Liar can look you in the eye and tell you absolute fabrications. Where is the report due today? "I gave my only copy to Word Processing, and they lost it." Did you call on General Tire on your business trip to Cincinnati? "I tried to, but the senior managers were tied up in a meeting." Yeah, sure.

The Liar wants the rewards of doing everything right while in fact doing most things wrong. Therefore, he or she is willing to lie in an effort to preserve appearances. And, sadly, the lies often work for years before tumbling down like a card castle. Fellow employees, even when they discover they've been deceived, usually grumble in silence instead of confronting the Liar. They may feel it's an exercise in frustration to try to pin the Liar down to the truth. He or she would probably squirm out by offering another lie.

Liars inevitably self-destruct in professional life, but on the way down cause untold damage to organizations and individuals. The white lies that "explain" a late lunch or missing supplies quickly turn into the huge lies that spell lost customers and litigation for the company.

At heart, the Liar usually has an almost phobic fear of failure—and that provides a starting place for his or her reclamation. The majority of business ventures at all levels are failures or only partial successes, even in the most profitable companies. Letters written to win new clients fail more often than succeed. Sales calls strike out more often than score. For successful professionals, failure isn't something to be ashamed of. It's the daily test of one's courage and ingenuity.

But the Liar doesn't understand failure and shortcomings. He or she treats failure like the plague; to admit to it is to threaten one's career, relationships, and self-image.

To salvage the career of the Liar in your organization, confront him or her with a glaring and indisputable untruth. Instead of allowing the Liar to go on to a litany of further prevarications and excuses, name the failure out loud: "John, the fact is that you didn't give the report to Word Processing. You never wrote the report." The Liar will probably respond with indignant huffing and puffing, with vague comments about "doubting my word." Again, make your point as clear as possible: "John, I am doubting your word. I don't think you're telling me the truth."

Eventually, the Liar will come around to an approximation of the truth: "Well, I thought if I admitted that I didn't finish the report you would think I was a flake." There. The Liar (perhaps for the first time in months or years) has admitted to his fear of failure. It's an ideal opportunity, assuming you want to help the Liar, to remind him that one failure doesn't necessarily sink a career. "John, you should have come to me and told me you just didn't get the report written on schedule. Wouldn't that be preferable to a series of lies?"

Strategy: Confront the Liar with a glaring untruth, then lead the conversation to the topic of how to handle failure. Occasional failures, while undesirable, are inevitable in anyone's career. Individuals with integrity face up to the failures and work to overcome them.

A Business Example

From a New York department store chain: "If you had a nickel for each white lie, gray lie, and black lie told in business every day, you could pay off the national debt. But that doesn't excuse lying; when lying hits close to home, it rankles. One of my buyers missed his bet badly on a volume purchase of sandals from Taiwan. The things were unstylish and of poor quality. When they hit the stores in late spring, they just sat there. So I asked my buyer what happened. He put on a shocked expression and said that the manufacturer had switched shipments on him. Those weren't the sandals he had ordered at all.

"Believing him, I got on the phone and blasted away at the manufacturer, a Taiwan company with whom we had done business for years. They denied making any error and sent me a copy of my buyer's original purchase order, which showed that he did, indeed, order the sandals shipped to us.

"I didn't care so much that my buyer had goofed—we all do—but that he lied to me. As a result of his lie, I risked a business relationship with a good supplier and made a fool of myself.

"The buyer and I had a long talk about what to do in the company when you goof. I think he understands now that lying is not an option."

S.O.P. NO. 8
THE BLAMER

Like the Liar, the Blamer has alienated virtually all of his or her social contacts in the company, and can't even claim the Liar's creativity to add credence to what he or she says. The Blamer is nothing if not predictable: faced with any question regarding his or her statements, actions, or responsibilities, the Blamer passes the ball to someone—anyone—within range. "I didn't get the letter sent to Mr. Jones because my secretary forgot to type it yesterday." This is a lie, of course; the letter was never given to the secretary to type. But it's a particularly dangerous form of lie because it places blame on an innocent party. The Blamer has not only given up any vestige of personal integrity but also has no regard for the reputations or welfare of others. If a secretary takes a bum rap for "forgetting" a letter, the Blamer breathes a sigh of relief for getting off the hook one more time.

Strategy: Because blaming is an insidious form of lying, use the confrontation technique to catch a Blamer in the act. Bring together the Blamer and the blamed party to arrive at the facts. The Blamer should be led to apologize to the person blamed. Repeat these gatherings as necessary until the Blamer recognizes the consequences of placing undeserved blame.

A Business Example

From a Milwaukee sports equipment manufacturer: "It began as a simple matter, but turned out to be a major personnel snafu. Someone in the company put the wrong grip on a shipment of 8,000 tennis rackets we sent out. The resulting recall would cost us about $11,000. When the error was reported by our retailers, I called my line foreman to find out what happened. He blamed the mistake on six line workers 'forced' upon him, he said, by the Personnel Department. The new workers weren't given enough training, he complained. No wonder they made such costly mistakes.

"Instead of letting the matter drop, I called the head of Personnel. She suggested that, together, we interview the six workers. I'm glad we did. Independently they reported that the incorrect grips were supplied to them in boxes by the foreman himself. It bothered me not only that the foreman would lie to me, but that he would endanger the jobs of six other people to save himself some embarrassment.

"When I confronted the foreman with the six employees' version of the situation, he called them liars. I let the matter drop after a short speech on the importance of telling the whole truth. But he's on notice that I'll follow up on his assignments of blame in the future."

S.O.P. NO. 9
THE BITTER RECLUSE

This difficult person has given up social contact in the company and all attempts at expression. The Recluse sits in an office making as few waves as possible, doing the bare minimum to maintain employment. In a silent, sullen way, the Recluse believes that he or she is paying the company back for some unnamed, galling offense. In some cases, there was in fact an event—perhaps a promotion turndown or denied raise—that sent the Recluse into hiding. But

often no such catalyst is present. The Recluse simply decides over time to hate work, hate coworkers, and hate the company. Instead of quitting, the Recluse may make a career out of doing as little as possible and saying nothing.

The Recluse is not a wallflower waiting for an invitation to dance, and few of the usual methods of socializing introverted employees work here. If asked to serve on a committee, the Recluse will forget most meetings and sit quietly in the back at meetings he or she does attend. If asked to lunch by a manager, the Recluse will make as little small talk as possible. Yes, I like my office. Yes, I like my coworkers. Everything is fine.

Breaking through to a Bitter Recluse requires energy and a bit of creativity on the part of a manager. The Recluse considers himself or herself to be a problem for the company, and feels inner satisfaction for the minor annoyances and irritations caused to others by such passive resistance. The Recluse becomes used to being treated as a problem. He or she knows the moves of that game well.

The challenge for a manager is to throw the Recluse off his or her game. Instead of treating the Recluse as a problem case ("Is anything the matter, Susan?"), the manager can switch roles and *become* the problem: "Susan, I'm facing a real problem and I need your help." Drawing the Recluse into business life as a solution-provider instead of as a problem can go far toward restoring this employee to a useful role.

A Business Example

From a San Diego U.S. post office: "People make jokes about working for the post office. But in general my fellow employees put in a solid day's work and take pride in a system that is improving each year. The jokes were accurate, however, about one employee waiting for retirement. Unfortunately, retirement in his case was still thirteen years away! He was absolutely bored stiff by his job, but wouldn't quit because of seniority and benefits. We used to joke with him about his lackluster attitude. He brought everyone down by his hangdog expression and depressed attitudes. The supervisor gave him special assignments from time to time, but nothing seemed to interest him. He was just an unhappy person who sat there like a piece of furniture. The rest of us had to ignore him if we were going to build any esprit d'corps among ourselves.

"This stalemate had a happy ending when a new supervisor gave him the title of 'troubleshooter' for the day shift. He really lit up when we went to him with particular problems, and he was usually pretty good in solving them. I guess he just wanted to feel needed."

ENCOURAGING PARTICIPATION AT MEETINGS

"Employees sometimes hold back for reasons that have more to do with how you're running the meeting than with their personality traits," says John Bray, president of The Forum Corporation of Boston. Bray is referring to the unconscious tendency of some managers to dominate discussion in an overwhelming way. Robert Bales, professor of psychology at Harvard University, points out that silent employees often feel they can't get a word in edgewise. "Your group probably includes a wide variety of personality types: dominant, submissive, friendly, unfriendly. Heavy talkers will compete with one another like wrestlers in a match. Don't expect more submissive people to insist on their way with heavy talkers."

WHEN CONFLICT IS BREWING WITH A DIFFICULT PERSON

These signs tell you that conflict is heating up:

◆ too much strong feeling attached to seemingly trivial topics

◆ rapidly shifting eyes or glaring

◆ name-calling and personal attacks

◆ implied or expressed threats

◆ expressions of panic, desperation, or despair

◆ needless harping on the same point

◆ an obvious effort to gather allies and set up opposed camps on an issue

◆ inappropriate use of biting humor and sarcasm

These signs tell you that parties are sidestepping potential conflict:

◆ unwillingness to discuss anything except "safe" topics

◆ premature agreement just to "keep the peace"

◆ letting others carry the ball

◆ silence from usually talkative members

◆ failure to move on to the next logical steps

◆ unwillingness to share information

◆ knowing glances and nonverbal cues

◆ recycling of old ideas

S.O.P NO. 10
THE ONE TRUE FRIEND

This difficult person, almost as socially isolated as the Bitter Recluse, attaches himself or herself (often unilaterally) to one or two other people in the organization. They hear far more than they wish of their One True Friend's complaints, rumor-mongering, and vendettas. When they suggest the One True Friend talk to management about these matters, they are answered silently by a shrug of the shoulder or a finger across the lips. Apparently, the One True Friend expects that his or her unwilling confidants will carry messages to the organizational grapevine or to authority figures in the company.

This rarely happens, of course. Those chosen by the One True Friend yawn or groan when he or she approaches for secretive disclosures. These embarrassing, frustrating encounters can lead the chosen to reject the One True Friend entirely or, more often, put up with his or her strange modes of communication out of pity.

The harm to an organization of One True Friend types lies not only in their inability to express their ideas but in the amount of time they waste for otherwise productive members of the company. Every half hour spent listening to the One True Friend is time stolen from more appropriate and more satisfying work on company time.

The goal in reclaiming and redirecting the energies of the One True Friend is to avoid punitive measures while encouraging wider social contacts. If those chosen by the One True Friend tell him or her to flake off, the result will benefit no one. The One True Friend will simply become another Bitter Recluse.

Strategy: Those chosen for special contact by the One True Friend should dignify his or her concerns by inviting in a larger group to hear the cries and whispers. The scenario works like this: The One True Friend approaches his or her designated listener for yet another monologue on what's wrong with the company, the project, and life itself. Instead of listening once again out of pity, the designated listener says, "Wait a minute. There are some other people who ought to hear what you're saying." Then, even over the One True Friend's protestations, the designated listener grabs any available bodies to broaden the audience to hear the One True Friend's secrets.

The result of this strategy is immediate and productive. The One True Friend edits his or her material for a broader and less patient audience. If there are matters of importance in the One True Friend's message, members of this broader audience can say so, and thereby draw this isolated person into a more valuable role on the team. In effect, the One True Friend learns that when he or she has something important to say, many people will want to hear it. But when he or she is simply blithering, all listeners fade away.

A Business Example

From an aerospace vice president: "At East Coast Aeronautics, Engineer Calvin Worth is known as a loner and an irascible old-timer—one of the employees who has been with the company since Day One. For all his eccentricities, however, Worth is a bona fide expert on some aspects of aeronautical hydraulics, particularly valves and seals. Like a latter-day Jeremiah, he shakes his head cynically about the work of others in these areas.

When the company prepared to deliver a revolutionary landing-gear apparatus to the Navy for its training jets, Calvin Worth pulled aside his designated listener, Linda Ying, for his usual pessimistic assessment: 'Mark my words, Linda, this gear is going to fail in heavy weather conditions. The hydraulics just haven't been worked out for...' Linda interrupted: 'Calvin, you need to get this information to people in the company who can do something with it. If you're right, they should pull back the product until we get it corrected.' But Calvin had his usual answer. 'No one listens to me. I'm just telling you because I don't want to stand by knowing what I do about the hydraulics and not telling anyone. They'll pay the price for not listening.'"

This scenario, of course, could end in several ways. Calvin could be wrong and only Linda's time would be abused. Or Calvin could be right, in which case both he and Linda are guilty in different degrees of not bringing this information forward. Finally, Calvin could be right and Linda may succeed in encouraging him to let others know about his dire warnings.

In fact, the East Coast Aeronautics example is not dissimilar from the interpersonal dynamics at the heart of the "O" ring disaster in equipment developed by Morton Thiokol for the Challenger space shuttle. As reported widely by CBS's "Sixty Minutes," two relatively isolated engineers raised questions about the stability of "O" rings under cold weather conditions prior to the shuttle's launch. In spite of warnings to coworkers and memos written by these engineers, the message never got through with sufficient urgency to the decision makers who needed to hear it.

S.O.P. NO. 11
THE STAR CHAMBER

Like the notorious 16th century English high-court judges for which they are named, these employees form a secretive clique that criticizes more than it contributes. In effect, these group members consider themselves the "silent minority" that functions to judge, often arbitrarily, the efforts of others.

A Star Chamber within a company can most easily be recognized as a group of employees who think alike, act together, and rarely explain their position. In too many firms, decision makers have learned to steer around these impediments, reasoning that it's best

"not to make them mad," to avoid a scene. As a consequence, weak decisions on the part of hamstrung leadership end up strengthening the power of the Star Chamber. Like a fat, immobile front line in football, these employees come to pride themselves on the fact that nothing gets by us. They rely on their mass, not their mission, to pursue their interests and thwart change.

Strategy: The Star Chamber can be dissolved by forcing its members to explain their judgments, resistance, and obstinacy in a public forum. This is best accomplished in quality circles or focus groups containing only a few members of the Star Chamber and many members from other constituencies. Without their buddies for silent support, members of the Star Chamber must find their own words to explain their actions and feelings. Inevitably, they discover that they *do* have positive contributions to make to ongoing dialogue on projects and processes—and that their newfound voice doesn't always harmonize well with the rest of the Star Chamber.

A Business Example

From Richard Allen, the new owner of Tropicale Restaurant in Los Angeles: "I inherited with my purchase of the restaurant a wait staff used to doing things their own way. Of the ten regular waiters, six in particular formed a Star Chamber that resisted my ideas for upgrading the way patrons were greeted and treated.

"For example, at one point I assembled the entire wait staff for a training meeting. I wanted to demonstrate how specials could be described and wines recommended to guests by the waiters. (Previously the waiters had plunked a "Specials" board on the table and asked, 'Any questions?') Halfway through the training session I noticed the Star Chamber group sending obvious nonverbal signals of resistance: rolling eyes, sour expressions, and knowing looks to one another. Especially for this group, the training session had little effect. Unless I was watching or within earshot, they continued to treat guests as brusquely and unprofessionally as before."

Richard faced the options of firing more than half of his wait staff (a temptation, but not a sound business decision), putting up with their resistance, or finding a way to bring them over to his way of doing things. He asked the instructor of a hospitality management program at a local community college to allow his wait staff, in teams of two, to audit a few classes attended by students interested in restaurant management. The instructor gladly agreed—students would gain much from the experienced input of real-world waiters.

Although Richard himself did not attend the classes, the word quickly came back to him that his waiters were outdoing themselves in recommending to class members the "right" and "classy" way to treat restaurant guests. When students came into the restaurant to observe these upscale service techniques in practice, waiters quickly (and largely unconsciously) found themselves meeting and exceeding Richard's standards for improved service. The Star Chamber fell apart as waiters began to individually live up to their own visions of professionalism.

S.O.P. NO. 12
THE SILENT MARTYR

This difficult person is found at the opposite end of the social spectrum from the Bitter Recluse. Like the Recluse, the Silent Martyr has little to verbalize. But his or her actions speak volumes to a wide audience in the company. The Silent Martyr is the unhappy transfer employee, the demoted manager, the reassigned supervisor. They say little about their situation, but they implicitly invite everyone to watch them act out their anger against the company.

Those actions take many forms, including petty sabotage of company equipment or procedures, flagrant violations of basic company policies, obvious lack of respect for company leadership, and quiet mockery of other employees' motives and efforts. The Silent Martyr has decided to go down in flames, and wants as large an audience as possible. His or her reasons range from crude revenge to a subtle form of self-assertion. The Silent Martyr calculates that his or her downward course may reveal to other employees the underside of their professional lives. "They'll see that I was right all along" is the implication.

The Silent Martyr is among the most dangerous of difficult people for the company, because he or she has nothing to lose. Given no hope of recognition or advancement, the Silent Martyr sees no reason not to throw a bug or two into a computer program, forget to pass along important messages, or abuse expense accounts and sick leave. Nor does the Silent Martyr try to stop other discontents in the company from following these leads.

Managers must act decisively to isolate and monitor Silent Martyrs. These malcontents have an almost cancerous influence on the attitudes of other workers. If termination is not an option, Silent Martyrs should be placed in highly structured work environments where little long-term damage can be done to the company. A Silent Martyr, for example, could be assigned to a personnel survey assignment, but not to the computer room; to a minor analysis task, but not to a planning function; to a monitored production duty, but not quality control.

Strategy: Protect the company and its workers from the Silent Martyr by isolating him or her to highly structured, carefully monitored assignments.

A Business Example

From a Delaware paint plant manager: "Even though our plant is highly automated, there are dozens of points in the production process where a careless worker or vandal could cause big problems. And the more a worker knows about the process, the bigger the problems can become.

"We just terminated an employee who, over a period of six months, had been responsible for the mis-mixing of over $15,000 worth of paint. It's the classic case of an employee who got one poor performance appraisal and decided to pay the company back. We couldn't figure out how flowmeters were mysteriously set incorrectly and timers turned off in his work area. However, several employees heard this individual joking after work about 'throwing a monkey wrench' into the production process. We placed him in a new position where he could be observed at all hours without his knowledge. During this period we encountered no more sabotage. Luckily for all of us, he then decided to move to the West Coast. It's a difficult problem when you think you have an employee sabotaging the plant but you can't prove it."

SUMMING UP

1. Difficult personality types can be charted (as on page 51) by paying attention to how involved they are with others and how outspoken they are.

2. After you understand what makes a particularly difficult person tick, settle upon strategies (such as those recommended in the chapter) to minimize the person's destructive influence on the organization and maximize his or her potential for positive contributions.

3. Apply the lessons learned from the Business Examples in this chapter to your collection of difficult people.

Chapter 5

Winning in Difficult Situations

Difficult people are never so nettlesome as when they're anxious, under fire, or on the spot. This chapter discusses how to avoid blow-ups and achieve your business goals during performance appraisals, interviews, disciplinary conferences, terminations, and exit sessions.

THE PERFORMANCE APPRAISAL

The chances are good that you will be communicating less-than-happy news to difficult people in your organization during performance appraisals. How do you tell a troubled, temperamental person that his or her performance just doesn't measure up?

TECHNIQUE:

SHOW before you speak. Your performance appraisal is no doubt in written form, with categories marked with checks, measured by points, or written out in prose. Many managers make the mistake of delivering bad news verbally, eyeball to eyeball with the difficult person, instead of letting the figures do the talking. Compare the following two performance appraisal openings involving a manager and Cal, a hostile loner in the company:

(Verbal version)
Manager: Cal, I have to make you aware that you're well below adequate performance levels in five important categories: working

relations, which haven't improved since your run-ins last quarter with your supervisor; time management—you're still coming in late and apparently leaving early without permission—

Cal: *(cutting in angrily)* I'm not going to sit here and rehash something that happened months ago!

The confrontation begins.

(SHOW version)

Manager: Cal, I've completed your performance evaluation for this quarter, and it looks like this. *(gives Cal a copy of the evaluation and provides time for him to digest it)*

Manager: What do you see there that we should discuss? *(This gives Cal the leadership role in the discussion.)*

In the latter approach, the manager has two advantages. First, Cal can look down at a piece of paper while receiving bad news. Cal can choose his own moment to compose himself before he looks up to begin discussion. If the same information were communicated verbally, Cal's feelings would be much less controlled; the flash of anger, disappointment, or humiliation could touch off a fiery tirade. Second, Cal is in a position to choose the first item for discussion. Many employees in this situation choose a less highly charged item than their major failings. Cal, for example, might look over the evaluation form and, when asked what he wants to discuss, pick a relatively minor problem: "I don't understand this item about not completing my training courses." Or Cal, if he's particularly sullen, may simply accept the performance appraisal: "Okay, so now what? I sign this?" In either case, the manager has the option of going on to discuss Cal's major problem. But here's the point: the discussion has had a chance to begin on relatively nonexplosive grounds.

TECHNIQUE:

PRAISE in a structured way. Employees facing poor performance evaluations are not fools, and they don't appreciate being insulted by the "bad news sandwich"—unflattering news between insincere statements of encouragement. "It's great to see you, Alice. Here are eighteen reasons why we're thinking about firing you. Have a nice day." Granted, there is great merit in beginning difficult performance appraisals with praise and encouragement, when possible. Positive feedback provides a buffer for potential confrontation.

But praise loses its effectiveness if it sounds like a setup for the real business of the performance appraisal. Even if the bulk of the session will be spent on problems rather than progress, you can establish an advantageous interpersonal climate by choosing your initial words of praise carefully:

Not: "Before we begin, Cal, let me say that you've shown some progress in . . ."

Instead: "Cal, this performance evaluation has three parts. I'd like to begin by discussing areas in which you're making good progress. Then we'll talk about problem areas and conclude with some goal-setting for this next quarter."

When positive feedback is built in to the performance appraisal in this way, the employee does not feel manipulated. Consequently, there's a much better chance that the discussion will prove constructive rather than confrontational.

THE INTERVIEW

You're desperate to hire one more employee for your proposal writing team—someone who knows desktop publishing backwards and forwards. A big contract hangs in the balance.

But the selection interview you've arranged is going poorly. The job candidate is a difficult person, and nervous as well—but at this point you'd hire Ghenghis Khan to get the proposal done. The candidate just won't open up and talk. What's going wrong?

Faced with a reticent or socially awkward interviewee, a manager may unconsciously attempt to make the interview easier by asking yes/no questions: "Have you worked with QuarkXPress? Do you know PageMaker?" The candidate need only respond in single syllables. Thus, the manager never gets to know much about the candidate's work attitudes or personality.

TECHNIQUE:

Ask open-ended questions to draw out a difficult or reticent person. Here are ten tried-and-true questions that won't produce a mere nod or grunt:

1. Tell me about a challenge you faced in a previous job.

2. How do you like to be managed?

3. Where do you want to find yourself in a year (three years, etc.)?

4. What kind of people rub you the wrong way in work situations?

5. How do you deal with the stress of deadlines?

6. What types of work bring you the most satisfaction?

7. Tell me what you liked and didn't like about your previous job.

8. What matters most to you in your professional life?

9. What can you offer this company immediately upon being hired?

10. What skills or abilities can we help you develop?

THE DISCIPLINARY CONFERENCE

For managers who dislike emotional confrontations, the disciplinary conference can be a stressful experience. There's nothing fun about telling a person that he or she isn't measuring up. The responses to such news can range from protests to insults to tears.

The key to making disciplinary interviews bearable is to "break the script"—that script worked out in detail by difficult people over the course of their lives. It goes something like this in their minds: "The manager [vice principal, parent, etc.] will call me into the office. I'll sit down across the desk and listen to the charges against me. Then I'll give a piece of my mind . . ." That mental script has probably been acted out dozens of times by a difficult person. The manager who unwittingly plays along with this script puts himself or herself in direct line for a long accumulation of anger and frustration. As one Michigan personnel director told us, "When employees start whining, I sometimes feel like telling them, 'I'm not your father. This is business.' "

TECHNIQUE:

Break the employee's long mental script entitled "Getting in Trouble" by

◆ meeting in an unexpected place (the employee's office, a private lunch table, etc.) Choosing an unexpected location for a disciplinary conference can change attitudes and results.

◆ bringing along an extra person. When circumstances permit, you can underline the importance of the disciplinary conference simply by having an additional person sit in—your assistant, perhaps, or the employee's direct supervisor.

◆ picking the time of day with care. Disciplinary sessions right after lunch tend to be much more "mellow," less emotional, than those that take place during high-energy times (9 to 11 A.M.) or high-stress times (3 to 5 P.M.)

THE TERMINATION

The game is over. You've filed the appropriate papers, received approval from senior management, and the difficult employee is almost history. Now you just have to tell the person being let go.

It's always risky to deal with difficult people when they have nothing to lose, as at the moment of termination. More than one manager has had his or her ears blistered by personal invective, bizarre accusations, and memorable profanity.

Why chance it? By timing the notice of termination appropriately, you can avoid the trauma of verbal attacks and help the terminated employee maintain some dignity.

TECHNIQUE:

Present the initial communication of termination (or any significant bad news) in written form, appropriately formal and respectful in tone. Make sure the communication arrives at a time when the employee can read it and react to it in privacy. It would be foolish, for example, to place a notice of termination in the employee's mailbox at 10 A.M. It is better to wait until just before the quitting hour.

TECHNIQUE:

Be available to talk—but not immediately available. Work out the timing of the termination so that the employee can't storm into your office to tell you off. This isn't a cowardly action; it's a prudent management technique that protects you and gives the terminated employee time to cool down.

THE EXIT INTERVIEW

As a rule, difficult people change jobs more often than other employees. In exit interviews, therefore, you are likely to be talking to people who didn't fit your company's culture, who didn't work out, who have little reason to be cooperative.

Getting these employees to give you valuable information requires tact and creativity. Even the most cantankerous interviewee may be able to shed valuable light on internal company problems, procedures, and personality conflicts. The trick is to motivate exiting employees to share their insights.

TECHNIQUE:

Treat exiting employees like royalty. Instead of holding the exit interview in the least attractive cubicle available, reserve an executive office or conference room. Coffee or soft drinks may be appropriate. Even an investment of time and money in a lunch meeting may pay informational dividends for the company from exiting employees who have much to share.

TECHNIQUE:
Choose a nonthreatening exit interviewer not directly involved in the exiting employee's work life. In American corporations, a surprisingly high percentage of exit interviews are conducted by managers and supervisors close to the specific duties and staff interactions of the leaving employee. These interviews are costly for the company and produce more heat than light. Old arguments resurface and little information is shared or recorded. Therefore, it is better to choose an objective, neutral party who can listen to the exiting employee in a noninhibiting, nonjudgmental way.

TECHNIQUE:
Ensure confidentiality by presenting the interviewee with a written statement of how shared information will be handled by the com-

pany. Remember, this is an employee who, for a reason, has chosen to leave the company. Should this employee be expected to trust the verbal assurance of confidentiality from a company employee that he or she may not know well? Particularly for the exiting employee who plans to remain in the same industry, what's said in an exit interview can be professionally hazardous if not handled with respect for the employee's desire to remain anonymous. A written statement of company policy encourages the exiting employee to "tell it like it is."

TECHNIQUE:

Thank the employee in advance and in detail. The company's gratitude for valuable information can be an encouraging force, even for difficult employees who don't give a hang about the company. Consider this scenario, in which gratitude occurs *early* as a motivator:

Interviewer: Jack, we appreciate having this hour to talk with you. It's probably a hectic time for you, getting packed up here and gearing up for your new job. But you're in an excellent position to tell us things we need to know to improve working conditions and production quality here. We'd also value your opinion on the management styles of those who supervised you.

Winning with difficult people is never more important than in situations such as these.

HOW PEOPLE ATTEMPT TO ATTAIN INFLUENCE OVER ONE ANOTHER

Strategy 1: Assertion   The forceful putting forth of one's position

"I make my point loud and clear."

Strategy 2: Bargaining   An attempt to agree on reciprocal advantages

"You scratch my back and I'll scratch yours."

Strategy 3: Compromise   An agreement to make mutual sacrifices for the sake of settlement

"You give up that and I'll give up this."

Strategy 4: Deceit   Manipulation through untruths

"You have nothing to lose."

Strategy 5: Emotional Disguise   Pose supported by emotional pretending

"I couldn't be happier about your promotion."

Strategy 6: Emotional Manipulation   An attempt to change someone else's sincerely felt emotions

> *"You've got to look confident if we're going to
> pull this off."*

Strategy 7: Evasion   Sidestepping those who might disapprove of
one's actions

> *"What they don't know won't hurt them."*

Strategy 8: Fait Accompli   Pursuing one's interests in the face of
those who object

> *"I do what I want."*

Strategy 9: Hinting   Indirect suggestions of one's goals

> *"Psst. Remember what we talked about."*

Strategy 10: Persistence   Repetition of one's wishes

> *"Let me say it again: here's what I want."*

Strategy 11: Persuasion   An effort to convince another person
through emotional and ad hominem appeals

> *"How can you do this to me while I'm recovering
> from an illness?"*

Strategy 12: Reason   An effort to convince another person
through rational argument

> *"I deserve a raise for the following reasons."*

Strategy 13: Thought Manipulation   Implanting one's own ideas within another person so as to appear to be that person's own thoughts

> *"Here's my idea. Present it for us and we'll share the credit."*

Strategy 14: Expertise   Using superior knowledge or the reputation for superior knowledge in persuading another person

> *"As a Ph.D., I have expert judgment in this matter."*

Strategy 15: Threat   Pointing to the undesirable consequences of the person's failing to act in a certain way

> *"If you don't, there will be trouble."*

Based on Toni Falbo, *"Multidimensional Scaling of Power Strategies,"* Journal of Personality and Social Psychology, *1977, 8, 537–547.*

◆

SUMMING UP

1. Make the most of negative performance evaluations by *showing* evaluations to the person before commenting on them and structuring whatever praise you can include.

2. Hire the best from among the rest by asking open-ended questions that get the candidate talking most of the time and the interviewer listening most of the time.

3. Avoid mushroom clouds in disciplinary interviews by "breaking the script" of what the disciplined employee expects you to say.

4. Communicate termination news in a nonembarrassing way and at an opportune time. Make yourself available to talk, but only after tempers have cooled.

5. Conduct valuable exit interviews by choosing the right interviewer, ensuring confidentiality, and using gratitude as a motivator for full disclosure from the exiting employee.

Chapter 6

Writing Effectively
to Difficult People

Why write to S.O.P.'s? More than one manager has answered, "So I don't have to talk to them." While letters and memos cannot and should not replace personal interaction with difficult people, these forms of communication do present distinct advantages:

◆ Written communication can't be interrupted by objections. Letters and memos "have their say" no matter what the reader thinks of them.

◆ Written communication can be orderly in a way that oral communication usually is not. Major points can stand out as headings, minor points can be bulleted, and supporting data can be attached.

◆ Written communication has no eyes, gestures, or posture to give away mood, temper, or attitudes. Written messages are "pure" compared to the competing verbal and nonverbal cues that make up oral communication. Mixed messages are less likely to result.

TEN TECHNIQUES WHEN WRITING TO DIFFICULT PEOPLE

Technique 1
Give your writing a positive tone.

Not: "You failed to send . . ."

Instead: "Please send . . ."

Not: "You still have not complied with . . ."

Instead: "Please take a moment to . . ."

You can still take firm stands and set binding deadlines in such positive communications. Your use of positive instead of negative phrases is intended to motivate your reader to take action.

Technique 2
Prefer the "you" perspective to the "I" perspective.

Not: "I have several items that I want to talk to you about. I can meet at 10:30 A.M. next Tuesday."

Instead: "We need to meet to discuss several items. Is 10:30 A.M. next Tuesday good for you?"

Letters and memos written with this technique sound much less dictatorial and egotistical. Readers are less likely to feel bullied and more likely to feel persuaded.

Technique 3

Provide a buffer for highly charged or negative information.

Not: (at the beginning of a memo) "Your expense report has been rejected due to insufficient verification of lodging . . ."

Instead: (buffer added) "The company is now operating under a new set of submission guidelines for expense reports. Perhaps you had not seen these when you submitted your last expense report, which I must return to you temporarily for more information on lodging expenses."

Technique 4

Don't make explanations for negative news if those explanations serve to intensify the reader's frustration or disappointment.

Not: (from a credit rejection) "Your application for a Gold Card has not been approved. Our review of your credit history shows several unpaid balances at local merchants and a tax lien in the amount of $4,324 . . ."

(Note here that a polite turndown would be sufficient. The applicant does not want to read a laundry list of credit problems.)

Instead: "Thank you for applying for a Gold Card. We regret that, after reviewing your credit, we cannot issue the card at this time. If you wish additional information on this decision, please call 389-2893. When these credit problems are resolved, we would welcome your reapplication."

Technique 5

Conclude written messages with specific directions on what to do.

Not: (last sentence in a disciplinary memo) "I trust that I have made myself clear and that you will respond accordingly."

Instead: (last sentence in a disciplinary memo) "Please act now to correct the unsafe working conditions (listed above) in your sector. When repairs are concluded, call me (ext. 324) for inspection."

Readers, particularly those we've classed as difficult people, have an amazing ability to ignore the obvious at the end of letters and memos. These readers need—and often want—to have your agenda for them clearly spelled out.

Technique 6

Break out your action recommendations as separate bulleted or numbered items.

Not: (at the end of a long memo) "In summary, management will require you to attend a three-day workshop on leadership development, meet regularly with Kent Foster to assess changes in your management style, and lead focus groups attended by your employees and senior managers on improving morale in your work unit."

Instead: (at the end of a long memo) "In summary, senior management will require you to

◆ attend a three-day workshop on leadership development

◆ meet regularly with Kent Foster to assess changes in your management style

◆ lead focus groups attended by your employees and senior managers on improving morale in your work unit."

A series of instructions, points, or recommendations can easily get lost unless clearly formatted. Use bullets for separate items if they have no priority order. If a priority is intended, number the points.

Technique 7

Keep crucial sentences short and to the point.

Not: (from a letter) "You can see, Barry, how embarrassing your actions have been for the company and how much trouble they have put us to in trying to repair the company's reputation with its clients, particularly those who placed orders on the basis of the incorrect information you supplied to them."

(Notice how the point gets almost completely lost in this jungle of words.)

Instead: (from the same letter)

"Barry, your actions have embarrassed the company. At considerable cost, we're trying to repair our reputation with clients you misserved."

Observe this rule in business writing: Half as much says twice as much.

Technique 8

Use the person's name to personalize and highlight portions of your message.

Impersonal: "Please speak to Janet Thompson (ext. 298) to get her input on possible presenters for the upcoming convention."

Personal: "Jack, please speak to Janet Thompson (ext. 298) to get her input on possible presenters for the upcoming convention."

Particularly in "bad news" communications, use of the reader's name can inject a note of concern and fellow feeling without weakening the message itself.

Technique 9
Use the "double signature" to reinforce your message.

Consider the force of this complimentary close at the end of a letter giving firm directions:

> *Sincerely,*
>
> *Alma R. Derwent*
>
> *Alma R. Derwent*
> *Director of Operations*
>
> *Robert A. Smith*
>
> *Robert A. Smith*
> *Corporate Vice President*

Two signatures announce "serious" loud and clear to the reader. Consequently, the message itself need not be stated as assertively as might be necessary with a single signature.

Technique 10

Refrain from telling readers how they feel. They may not feel that way at all.

Not: (in a "bad news" memo) "I can imagine how disappointed you must feel at receiving this news, Barbara. You probably feel your work on the project has been totally unappreciated."

Instead: Simply omit the sentences. You can express *your* feelings, but don't presume to express the reader's.

FIVE MEMOS/LETTERS TO DIFFICULT PEOPLE ABOUT DIFFICULT SITUATIONS

(After the first letter, all other examples are formatted as memos. The texts of these memos, however, can serve as texts for letters as well.)

EXAMPLE NO. 1
LETTER INFORMING AN EMPLOYEE OF A COMPLAINT

*Aug. 12, 199_*
Mr. Nathan Miller
Sales Associate
BERTON HOME PRODUCTS, INC.
2893 Western Hwy.
Seattle, WA 98323

Dear Nathan:

On August 5, 199_, I received the enclosed letter from Ms. Paula Wilson of Bellevue. Please read her letter with care. In it, she alleges that you angrily insulted her when she asked for product locations in our Seattle #5 store.

I'm eager to hear your side of this matter so that I can communicate it to Ms. Wilson. From your Orientation Course last month you know how highly the company values the trust and friendship of its customers. We investigate all employee-related customer complaints closely.

Please call me (ext. 892) no later than Wednesday, August 14, for specific directions on how to proceed. Company policy requires both a written response from you and a conference, which I will attend. I look forward to working with you in straightening this matter out for all concerned.

Sincerely,
Richard B. Todd
Supervisor

EXAMPLE NO. 2
MEMO OF GROUP REORGANIZATION

To: All Employees, Unit C
From: Roberta Allen
*   General Manager*
Subject: Group reorganization effective March 1, 199_.
*Date: Feb. 15, 199_*

As I discussed with you in our meeting Feb. 1, senior management has been studying a reorganization plan affecting Unit C. At its meeting yesterday, the Executive Committee approved the merger of Unit C with Unit D.

While this change involves no layoffs, the leadership and reporting order in the new unit—identified as Unit E—will change significantly. I have attached a detailed organizational chart showing new positions and titles.

We plan, through this reorganization, on achieving a more cost-effective way of continuing the high quality of work for which both divisions have been known in the company.

On Friday, Feb. 19, we will meet in Conference Room A at 10 p.m. to deal with the many adjustments made necessary by this merger. In the meantime, contact me (ext. 982) if I can be helpful with individual concerns or questions.

EXAMPLE NO. 3
MEMO TURNING DOWN EMPLOYEE SUGGESTION

To: Bud Forrest
Director of Advertising
From: Rita Went
Vice President
*Subject: Response to your memo of Jan. 6, 199_*
*Date: Jan. 8, 199_*

I gave considerable thought to your suggestion for a revised pro-motional package to accompany the TR-8A project. While I think your proposal has many strengths, I must turn it down for now for budgetary reasons. Let's remember to meet early in the new fiscal year to give it a second look.

Thanks, however, for the initiative and hard work you showed in putting the revision proposal together.

EXAMPLE NO. 4
MEMO DECLINING AN INVITATION

To: Gwen Richfield
Chair, Convention Planning Committee
From: Oliver Polt
Manager, Computer Division

Subject: Your speaking invitation
*Date: Sept. 7, 199_*

I appreciated being selected as a convention speaker by your committee, Gwen. I know how hard you have all been working to put together a valuable meeting.

However, during the ten days prior to the convention, I'm scheduled to represent the company at a trade show in Europe. Therefore, I must respectfully decline your invitation; both my preparation time and my stamina would be in short supply.

If I can be of help in another way before the meeting, please give me a call (ext. 982).

EXAMPLE NO. 5
MEMO TAKING RESPONSIBILITY FOR A MISTAKE

To: Ronald R. Samworth
   Vice President
From: Everett Thompson
   Supervisor 3
Subject: Items missing from Storage Room D
*Date: May 4, 199_*

As you know, Storage Room D was discovered unlocked on Tuesday morning, May 2. We've now completed a complete inventory of contents, with the following result:

[Missing items]

* 16 reams of photocopy paper
* 2 cases (24 units) of IBM typewriter ribbon
* 6 Hewlett Packard LaserJet II ink cartridges

* 3 cases (144 items) of general purpose pens
* 6 rolls of FAX paper

While I don't know who left the storage room unlocked, I do recognize that it's my responsibility to check the door each evening before leaving the building. I didn't do so on Monday evening, May 1, and therefore accept responsibility for this unfortunate incident.

I am continuing an internal investigation to find the person(s) involved in the theft. As more information becomes available, I'll be in touch immediately. Again, I'm sorry for my mistake.

IN CONCLUSION

Unless you move to a desert island, you will probably never escape difficult people in your professional life.

So why not win with difficult people? By understanding what makes them tick, you can understand why you get ticked off. By understanding yourself, you can get the most out of even the most stressful of your business relationships.

CHARACTERISTICS OF BELIEVABLE COMMUNICATION

1. Owning up to positions

    Yes "I don't think your proposal will work because . . ."

    No "Your proposal may run into some problems upstairs—you know how they are . . ."

2. Emotionally honest

    Yes "I was disappointed when you failed to show for that meeting . . ."

    No "Mad? Me? Why do you think I should be mad?"

3. Accepting

    Yes "Thanks for the suggestion. Let's investigate its possibilities."

    No "Just leave the conceptual stuff to me."

4. Focused

    Yes "I think you should reconsider my application."

    No "You don't take time to really read anything on your desk."

5. Unselfish

    Yes "I have some thoughts on the merger. What do you think?"

    No "Wait a minute, wait a minute. I've been through all this before. Here's what I think."

6. Evidence-oriented
Yes "I understand that you told our client X, Y, and Z."
No "I hear you've been lying to our client again."

7. Respectful
Yes "I'm interested in hearing your perspective."
No "As a secretary, you just wouldn't understand these matters."

8. Appropriate Level of Intimacy
Yes "We've known each other for a couple months and I've been feeling a certain amount of tension in our working relations."
No (same relationship) "Do you have some home problems or something? I don't feel that you're doing much to build a friendship between us here at work."

SUMMING UP

1. Win with difficult people through your writing by choosing positive language and emphasizing the "you" perspective.

2. Lessen the negative effects of bad news by using a buffer statement and, when appropriate, omitting lengthy and self-justifying explanations for the unfavorable news you are communicating.

3. Achieve your objective by providing specific directions on what you want the reader to do. Do not, however, tell readers how they "must feel."

4. Keep your main message short and to the point. Use the person's name to attract attention to your message and personalize it.

SUGGESTED READING

Brinkman, Dr. Rich and Dr. Rick Kirschner. *Dealing with People You Can't Stand (How to Bring Out the Best in People at Their Worst)*. New York: McGraw-Hill, 1994.

Felder, Leonard, Ph.D. *Does Someone at Work Treat You Badly?* New York: Berkeley Business, 1993.

Guzzo, Richard A. and Eduardo Salas & Associates. *Team Effectiveness and Decision Making Organizations*. San Francisco: Jossey Bass, 1995.

Mainz, Charles C. and Henry P. Sims, Jr. *Business without Bosses*. New York: John Wiley & Sons, 1993.

Musgrave, James and Michael Annis. *Relationship Dynamics*. New York: The Free Press (Simon & Schuster), 1996.

Potter, Dr. Beverly. *From Conflict to Cooperation (How to Mediate a Dispute)*. Berkeley: Ronin Press, 1996.

Ralston, Faith, Ph.D. *Hidden Dynamics (How Emotions Can Affect Business Performance & How You Can Harness Their Power for Positive Results)*. New York: AMACOM, 1995.

Stevenson, William J. *Production Operations Management*. Burr Ridge, IL: IRWIN, Inc., 1993.

Tulgam, Bruce. *Managing Generation X*. Santa Monica: Merrit, 1995.

Weeks, Dudley, Ph.D. *Eight Essential Steps to Conflict Resolution*. New York: Jeremy P. Tarcher (Putnam), 1996.

Wheatley, Margaret. *Leadership and the New Science (Learning About Organizations from an Orderly Universe)*. San Francisco: Bennett Koehler Publishers, 1994.

Wilms, Welford W. *Restoring Prosperity: How Workers and Managers Are Forging a New Culture of Cooperation.* New York: Random House, 1996.

INDEX

More selected BARRON'S titles:

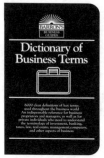
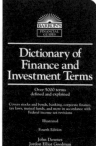

BARRON'S BUSINESS KEYS Each "key" explains approximately 50 concepts and provides a glossary and index. Each book: Paperback, approx. 160 pp., 4 3/16" x 7", $4.95, Can. $6.50.

Keys for Women Starting or Owning a Business (4609-9)
Keys to Avoiding Probate and Reducing Estate Taxes (4668-4)
Keys to Business and Personal Financial Statements (4622-6)
Keys to Buying a Foreclosed Home (4765-6)
Keys to Buying a Franchise (4484-3)
Keys to Buying and Owning a Home, 2nd Edition (9032-2)
Keys to Buying and Selling a Business (4430-4)
Keys to Choosing a Financial Specialist (4545-9)
Keys to Conservative Investments, 2nd Edition (9006-3)
Keys to Estate Planning and Trusts, 2nd Edition (1710-2)
Keys to Financing a College Education, 2nd Edition (1634-3)
Keys to Improving Your Return on Investments (ROI) (4641-2)
Keys to Incorporating, 2nd Edition (9055-1)
Keys to Investing in Common Stocks, 2nd Edition (9004-7)
Keys to Investing in Corporate Bonds (4386-3)
Keys to Investing in Government Securities, 2nd Edition (9150-7)
Keys to Investing in International Stocks (4759-1)
Keys to Investing in Municipal Bonds (9515-4)
Keys to Investing in Mutual Funds, 3rd Edition (9644-4)
Keys to Investing in Options and Futures, 2nd Edition (9005-5)
Keys to Investing in Real Estate, 2nd Edition (1435-9)
Keys to Investing in Your 401(K) (1873-7)
Keys to Managing Your Cash Flow (4755-9)
Keys to Mortgage Financing and Refinancing, 2nd Edition (1436-7)
Keys to Personal Financial Planning, 2nd Edition (1919-9)
Keys to Personal Insurance (4922-5)
Keys to Purchasing a Condo or a Co-op (4218-2)
Keys to Reading an Annual Report, 2nd Edition (9240-6)
Keys to Retirement Planning, 2nd Edition (9013-6)
Keys to Risks and Rewards of Penny Stocks (4300-6)
Keys to Saving Money on Income Taxes, 2nd Edition (9012-8)
Keys to Starting a Small Business (4487-8)
Keys to Starting an Export Business (9600-2)
Keys to Surviving a Tax Audit (4513-0)
Keys to Understanding Bankruptcy, 2nd Edition (1817-6)
Keys to Understanding the Financial News, 2nd Edition (1694-7)
Keys to Understanding Securities (4229-8)
Keys to Women's Basic Professional Needs (4608-0)

Available at bookstores, or by mail from Barron's. Enclose check or money order for full amount plus sales tax where applicable and 15% for postage & handling (minimum charge $4.95). Prices subject to change without notice. $= U.S. dollars • Can. $= Canadian dollars • Barron's ISBN Prefix 0-8120

Barron's Educational Series, Inc.
250 Wireless Boulevard • Hauppauge, NY 11788
In Canada: Georgetown Book Warehouse
34 Armstrong Avenue, Georgetown, Ont. L7G 4R9

(#10) R 6/97